C. H. Spurgeon

Spurgeon's Sermons
on
Christmas
and Easter

CHARLES HADDON SPURGEON

kregel
PUBLICATIONS

Grand Rapids, MI 49501

Spurgeon's Sermons on Christmas and Easter
by Charles H. Spurgeon.

Copyright © 1995 by Kregel Publications.

Published by Kregel Publications, a division of Kregel, Inc., P.O. Box 2607, Grand Rapids, MI 49501. Kregel Publications provides trusted, biblical publications for Christian growth and service. Your comments and suggestions are valued.

Cover artwork: Don Ellens
Cover and book design: Alan G. Hartman

Library of Congress Cataloging-in-Publication Data

Spurgeon, C. H. (Charles Haddon), 1834–1892.
  [Sermons on Christmas and Easter]
  Spurgeon's Sermons on Christmas and Easter / by Charles H. Spurgeon.
     p.   cm.—(C.H. Spurgeon sermon series)
    1. Christmas sermons. 2. Easter—Sermons.
3. Baptists—Sermons. 4. Sermons, English. I. Title. II. Series: Spurgeon, C. H. (Charles Haddon), 1834–1892. C. H. Spurgeon sermon series.
BV4257.S65   1995   252'.61—dc20   95-17319
                                      CIP

ISBN 0-8254-3689-3 (pbk.)

1 2 3 4 5 printing / year 99 98 97 96 95

Printed in the United States of America

Contents

1

Immanuel—the Light of Life

Nevertheless the dimness shall not be such as was in her vexation, when at the first he lightly afflicted the land of Zebulun and the land of Naphtali, and afterward did more grievously afflict her by the way of the sea, beyond Jordan, in Galilee of the nations. The people that walked in darkness have seen a great light: they that dwell in the land of the shadow of death, upon them hath the light shined (Isaiah 9:1–2).

As in this case the Revised Version is much to be preferred, we will now read it:

But there shall be no gloom to her that was in anguish. In the former time he brought into contempt the land of Zebulun and the land of Naphtali, but in the latter time hath he made it glorious, by the way of the sea, beyond Jordan, Galilee of the nations. The people that walked in darkness have seen a great light: they that dwelt in the land of the shadow of death, upon them hath the light shined (Isaiah 9:1–2).

When Judah was in sore distress, the sign that she should be delivered was Immanuel. "Behold, a virgin shall conceive, and bear a son, and shall call his name Immanuel" (Isaiah 7:14). When no other ray of comfort could be found, light came from the promise of the wondrous birth of Him whose name is "God with us." God alone would be the deliverer of Judah when overmatched by her two enemies. God would be with them, and He gave them as a pledge a vision of that time when, in very deed, God would dwell among men, and wear their nature in the person of the Virgin-born.

It is noteworthy that the clearest promises of the Messiah have been given in the darkest hours of history. If the prophets had been silent

---

This sermon was taken from *The Metropolitan Tabernacle Pulpit* and was preached on Sunday morning, September 14, 1890.

upon the coming One before, they always speak out in the cloudy and dark day; for well the Spirit made them know that the coming of God in human flesh is the lone star of the world's night. It was so in the beginning, when our first parents had sinned, and were doomed to quit the Paradise of delights. It was not meet that rebels should be dwellers in the garden of the Lord, they must go forth to till the ground from whence they were taken; but before they went, there fell upon their ears the prophecy of the Deliverer who would be born: "The seed of the woman shall bruise the serpent's head."

How bright shone that one promise amid the surrounding gloom! The earliest believers found in this hope of the coming Conqueror of the serpent a solace amid their labor and sorrow. When Israel was in Egypt, when they were in the sorest bondage, and when many plagues had been wrought on Pharaoh, apparently without success—for he knew not the Lord, neither would he let His people go—then Israel saw the Messiah set before her as the Paschal lamb, whose blood sprinkled on the lintel and the two side posts secured the chosen from the avenger of blood. The type is marvelously clear, and the times were marvelously dark. It seemed as if the Lord would make the consolation to abound even as the tribulation abounded.

I will not multiply instances; but I will quote three cases from the prophetical books which now lie open before us. In Isaiah 28:16 you read that glorious prophecy: "Behold, I lay in Zion for a foundation a stone, a tried stone, a precious corner stone, a sure foundation: he that believeth shall not make haste." When was that given? It was pronounced when the foundation of society in Israel was rotten with iniquity, and when its cornerstone was oppression. Read from verse 14: "Wherefore hear the word of the Lord, ye scornful men, that rule this people which is in Jerusalem. Because ye have said, We have made a covenant with death, and with hell are we at agreement; when the overflowing scourge shall pass through, it shall not come unto us: for we have made lies our refuge, and under falsehood have we hid ourselves." Thus, when lies and falsehoods ruled the hour, the Lord proclaims the blessed truth that the Messiah would come and would be a sure foundation for believers.

Next, look, into Jeremiah, and pause at the twenty-third chapter and the fifth verse: "Behold, the days come, saith the LORD, that I will raise unto David a righteous Branch, and a King shall reign and prosper, and shall execute judgment and justice in the earth. In his days Judah shall be saved, and Israel shall dwell safely: and this is his name whereby he shall be called, THE LORD OUR RIGHTEOUSNESS." When was this clear testimony given? Read the former verses of the chapter, and see that the pastors were destroying and scattering the sheep of Jehovah's pasture. When the people of the Lord thus found their worst enemies where they ought to have met with friendly care, then they were promised happier days through the coming of the divine Son of David. I will only further detain you while we glance at Ezekiel 34:23, where the Lord says, "And I will set up one shepherd over them, and he shall feed them, even my servant David; he shall feed them, and he shall be their shepherd." When came this cheering promise concerning that great Shepherd of the sheep? It came when Israel is thus described: "And they were scattered, because there is no shepherd: and they became meat to all the beasts of the field, when they were scattered. My sheep wandered through all the mountains, and upon every high hill: yea, my flock was scattered upon all the face of the earth, and none did search or seek after them." Thus you see that, in each case, when things were at their worst, the Lord Jesus was the one well of consolation in a desert of sorrows.

> Midst darkest shades, if he appear,
> Our dawning has begun;
> He is our soul's bright morning star,
> And he our rising sun.

In the worst times we are to preach Christ, and to look to Christ. In Jesus there is a remedy for the direst of diseases, and a rescue from the darkest of despairs.

Ahaz, as the chapter tells us, was in great danger, for he was attacked by two kings, each one stronger than he; but the Lord promised him deliverance, and commanded him to choose a sign either in the heights, or in the depths. This, under a hypocritical pretense, he refused to do; and therefore the Lord chose as his own token the appearance of the heavenly Deliverer, who would be God, and yet born of a woman. "Behold, a virgin shall conceive, and bear a son, and shall call his name Immanuel." He was to eat butter and honey, like other children in that land of milk and honey, and yet he was to be the Mighty God, the Everlasting Father, the Prince of Peace. We see here Godhead in union with manhood. We behold Jesus, man "of the substance of his mother," and yet "God over all, blessed for ever." Surely this God-appointed sign was both in the depth and in the height above: the Man of sorrows, the Son of the Highest.

This vision was the light of the age of Ahaz. It is God's comfort to troubled hearts in all the ages; it is God's sign of grace to us this morning. The sure hope of sinners and the great joy of saints is the incarnate Lord, Immanuel, God with us. May He be your joy and mine even this day. He it is who is the great light of the people who dwell in the land of the shadow of death: if any among you are in that dreary land, may He be light and life to you! He alone could make the darkness of Zebulun and Naphtali to disappear in a blaze of glory: He can do the same for those who sorrow at this hour.

Now, if I may have your patient attention, I shall, as I am enabled, *illustrate this fact by the context.* Scripture best explains Scripture, as diamond cuts diamond. The Word of God carries its own keys for all its locks. It is profitable to study Scripture, not in fragments, but in connected paragraphs. It is well to see the glory of a star, but better to behold the whole constellation in which it shines. When I have dwelt upon the context, I shall, in the second place, *press home certain joyful truths connected with the subject.*

There is to be a light breaking in upon the sons of men who sit in darkness, and this light is to be found only in the incarnate God.

Illustration of This Fact of Light by the Context

I must carry you back to the fourteenth verse of the seventh chapter. *The sign of coming light is Jesus.* "Therefore the Lord himself shall give you a sign; Behold, a virgin shall conceive, and bear a son, and shall call his name Immanuel." In Judah's trouble, the Virgin-born was God's token that He would deliver, and that speedily; for in less time than it would take such a child to reach years of knowledge, both Judah's royal adversaries would be gone.

The sign was good for Ahaz; but it is better far for us. Behold the incarnate Son of God born of Mary at Bethlehem; what can this intend for us but grace? If the Lord had meant to destroy us, He would not have assumed our nature. If He had not been moved with mighty love to a guilty race, He would never have taken upon Himself their flesh and blood. It is a miracle of miracles that the Infinite should become an infant; that He who is pure spirit, and fills all things, should be wrapped in swaddling bands, and cradled in a manger. He took not on Him the nature of angels, though that would have been a tremendous stoop from Deity, but He descended lower still; for He took on Him the seed of Abraham. "He was made in all things like unto his brethren"; though "he counted it not robbery to be equal with God." It is not in the power of human lips to speak out all the comfort which this one sign contains. If any troubled soul will look believingly at God in human flesh, he must take heart of hope. If he looks believingly, his comfort will come right speedily. The birth of Jesus is the proof of the good will of God to men: I am unable to conceive of proof more sure. He would not have come here to be born among men, to live among them, to suffer and to die for them, if He had been slow to pardon, or unwilling to save. O despairing soul, does not Immanuel, God with us, make it hard to doubt the mercy of the Lord?

We have comfort in the fact that our Lord was truly man. He whom we worship became one with us in nature. He was born as other children are born, save that His mother was a virgin. He was fed as other children were fed, upon curds and honey, the food of a pastoral country. He had to be developed, as to His natural powers, even as other little ones. He grew up from childhood to youth, and from youth to manhood, passing through all the gradations of human weakness, even as we have done; and He was obedient to His parents, even as other children should be. He is, therefore, really and truly a man; and this fact is a bright particular star for sinners' eyes.

Come to Jesus, you who languish under terror and dread because of the majesty of Deity; for here you see how compassionate He is, how sympathetic He can be, yes, how near of kin He has become. He is God; but He is God *with us*. He is bone of our bone, and flesh of our flesh, a brother born for adversity; and here the most trembling may be at rest. God in our nature is a grand prophecy of salvation and bliss for us. Why has He come down to us but that we may come up to Him? Why has He taken our nature in its sorrow, but that we may be made partakers of the divine nature in righteousness and holiness? He comes down, not to thrust us lower, but to lift us to heights of perfectness and glory. That Jesus is man and yet God, is full of hope and joy for us who believe in Him. I do not feel as if I wanted to enlarge upon this glorious truth with words alone. Oh, that the Holy Spirit would convey to each one of my hearers the light which shines from the star of incarnation! Oh, that at this moment the people who walk in darkness may see in the incarnate God a great light, and perceive in Him the prophecy and assurance of all good things! Not long shall evil oppress the believer; for in Christ Jesus God is with us; and if God be for us, who can be against us?

> O joy! there sitteth in our flesh,
>   Upon a throne of light,
> One of a human mother born,
>   In perfect Godhead bright!
>
> For ever God, for ever man,
>   My Jesus shall endure;
> And fix'd on him, my hope remains
>   Eternally secure.

Further on we see our Lord Jesus as *the hold-fast of the soul in time of darkness*. See in the eighth verse of the eighth chapter the whole country overwhelmed by the fierce armies of the Assyrians, as when a land is submerged beneath a flood. Then you read—"And he shall pass through Judah; he shall overflow and go over, he shall reach even to the neck; and the stretching out of his wings shall fill the breadth of thy land, O Immanuel." The one hope that remained for Judah was that her country was Immanuel's land. There would Immanuel be born, there would He labor, and there would He die. He was by eternal covenant the King of that land, and no Assyrian could keep still "thy land, O Immanuel!"

If, my dear friend, you are a believer in Christ, you belong to Him, and you always were His by sovereign right, even when the Enemy held you in possession. The Devil had set his mark upon you, so that you might be forever his branded slave; but he had no legal right to you, for Immanuel had redeemed you, and He claimed you as His own. Had we known, we might exultingly have gloried over you, "Thy soul, O Immanuel!" The Father gave you to Jesus, and Jesus Himself bought you with His blood; and, though you knew it not, He had the title deeds of you, and would not lose His inheritance. Herein lay your hope when all other hope was gone. Herein is your hope now. If you belong to Jesus, He will have you. If He bought you with His blood, He will not shed that blood in vain. If on the cross He bore your sin, He will not suffer you to bear it, and so to make void His sacrifice. If you belong to Him He will deliver you, even as David snatched the lamb of His flock from the jaw of the lion and the paw of the bear.

O sinner, this is the great hope we have for you: if you were given of old to Jesus He will rescue you from the hand of the Enemy. This, also, is your own hope: if you believe in Jesus you belong to Jesus; if you trust Him, He has redeemed you with a price, and will also redeem you with power. If you cast your guilty soul at His dear feet, and take Him to be your own Savior, you are not your own, but bought with a price; and sooner shall heaven and earth pass away than one whom Jesus calls His own shall be left to perish. "Having loved His own, He loved them unto the end." Immanuel, God with us, is strong to rescue His own out of the Enemy's hand.

Further on in the chapter we learn that Jesus is *our star of hope as to the destruction of the Enemy*. The foes of God's people shall be surely vanquished and destroyed because of Immanuel. Note well, in verses 9 and 10, how it is put twice over, like an exultant taunt: "Gird yourselves, and ye shall be broken in pieces; gird yourselves, and ye shall be broken in pieces. Take counsel together, and it shall come to nought; speak the word, and it shall not stand: for Immanuel." Our version translates the word into "God with us," but it is "Immanuel." In Him, even in our Lord Jesus Christ, dwelleth all the fullness of the Godhead bodily, and He has brought all that Godhead to bear upon the overthrow of the foes of His people. Let the powers of darkness consult and plot as they may, they can never destroy the Lord's redeemed. Lo! I see councils of evil spirits: they sit down in Pandemonium, and conspire to ruin a soul redeemed by blood. They lay their heads together, they use a cunning deep as hell; they are eager to destroy the soul that rests in

Jesus. In vain their devices, for the incarnate God is embodied wisdom. Now see them: they rise from the council table, they put on their harnesses; their arrows are dipped in malice, and their bows are strong to shoot afar. Each foul spirit takes his sword, his sharp sword, that will cut a soul to the center, and kill it with despair; but their weapons shall all fail. If we fly to Jesus, who is God with us, no weapon that is formed against us shall prosper. His name Immanuel is the terror of the hosts of hell. God with us means confusion to our foes. As the death of death, and hell's destruction, our Immanuel cries to the legions of the pit, "Gird yourselves, and ye shall be broken in pieces. Gird yourselves, and ye shall be broken in pieces"! Let us take courage and defy the legions of darkness. Let us charge them with this war cry, "God is with us." Immanuel, who has espoused our cause, is God Himself, almighty to save: the enemies of our souls shall be trodden under His feet, and He shall bruise Satan even under our feet shortly. Satan from the first hated God in our nature, for thus man was exalted beyond the angels; and this his pride could not endure. The Lord Jesus is as the star Wormwood to our spiritual adversaries, rousing their fiercest hate, and foreboding their sure overthrow.

Further on we find *the Lord Jesus as the morning light after a night of darkness*. The last verses of the eighth chapter picture a horrible state of wretchedness and despair: "And they shall pass through it, hardly bestead and hungry: and it shall come to pass, that when, they shall be hungry, they shall fret themselves, and curse their king and their God, and look upward. And they shall look unto the earth; and behold trouble and darkness, dimness of anguish; and they shall be driven to darkness." But see what a change awaits them! Read the fine translation of the Revised Version: "But there shall be no gloom to her that was in anguish." What a marvelous light from the midst of a dreadful darkness! It is an astounding change, such as only God with us could work. Many of you know nothing about the miseries described in those verses, but there are some here who have traversed that terrible wilderness, and I am going to speak to them. I know where you are this morning: you are being driven as captives into the land of despair, and for the last few months you have been tramping along a painful road, "hardly bestead [situated] and hungry." You are sorely put to it, and your soul finds no food of comfort, but is ready to faint and die. You fret yourself: your heart is wearing away with care and grief and hopelessness. In the bitterness of your soul you are ready to curse the day of your birth. The captive Israelites cursed their king who had led them into their defeat and bondage; in the fury of their agony, they even cursed God and longed to die. It may be that your heart is in such a ferment of grief that you know not what you think, but are like a man at his wits' end. Those who led you into sin are bitterly remembered; and as you think upon God you are troubled. This is a dreadful case for a soul to be in, and it involves a world of sin and misery. You look up, but the heavens are as brass above your head; your prayers appear to be shut out from God's ear; you look around you upon the earth, and behold "trouble and darkness, and dimness of anguish"; your every hope is slain, and your heart is torn asunder with remorse and dread. Every hour you seem to be hurried by an irresistible power into greater darkness, yes, even into the eternal midnight. In such a case none can give you comfort save Immanuel, God with us. Only God, espousing your cause, and bearing your sin, can possibly save you. See, He comes for your salvation! Behold, He has come to seek and to save that which was lost. God has come down from heaven, and veiled Himself in our flesh, that He might be able to save to the uttermost. He can save the chief of sinners: He can save you.

Come to Jesus, you that have gone furthest into transgression, you that sit down in despondency, you that shut yourselves up in the iron cage of despair. For such as you there shines this star of the first magnitude. Jesus has appeared to save, and He is God and man in one person: man that He may feel our woes, God that He may help us out of them. No minister can save you, no priest can save you—you know this right well; but here is one who is able to save to the uttermost, for He is God as well as man. The great God is good at a dead lift; when everything else has failed, the lever of omnipotence can lift a world of sin. Jesus is almighty to save! That which in itself is impossibility is possible with God. Sin which nothing else can remove is blotted out by the blood of Immanuel. Immanuel, our Savior, is God with us; and God with us means difficulty removed, and a perfect work accomplished. But I fail to tell you in words. Oh, that the light itself would shine into your souls, that those of you who have as yet no hope may see a great light, and may from henceforth be of good courage!

Once more, dear friends, we learn from that which follows our text, that *the reign of Jesus is the star of the golden future.* He came to Galilee of the Gentiles, and made that country glorious which had been brought into contempt. That corner of Palestine had very often born the brunt of invasion, and had felt more than any other region the edge of the keen Assyrian sword. They were at first troubled when the Assyrian was bought off with a thousand talents of silver; but they were more heavily afflicted when Tiglath-pileser carried them all away to Assyria, for which see the fifteenth chapter of the second book of the Kings. It was a wretched land, with a mixed population, despised by the purer race of Jews; but that very country became glorious with the presence of the incarnate God. It was there that all manner of diseases were healed; there the seas were stilled, and the multitudes were fed; it was there that the Lord Jesus found His apostles, and there He met the whole company of His followers when He had risen from the dead. That first land to be invaded by the enemy was made the headquarters of the army of salvation: this very Zebulun and Naphtali, which had been so downtrodden and despised, was made the scene of the mighty works of the Son of God. Even so, at this day His gracious presence is the daydawn of our joy.

If Christ comes to you, my dear hearer, as God with us, then shall your joy be great; for you shall joy as with the joy of harvest, and as those rejoice that divide the spoil. Is it not so? Many of us can bear our witness that there is no joy like that which Jesus brings. Here read and interpret the third verse of the ninth chapter.

Then shall your enemy be defeated, as in the day of Midian. Gideon was, in his dream, likened to a barley cake, which struck the tent of Midian, so that it lay along. He and his few heroes, with their pitchers and their trumpets, stood and shouted, "The sword of the Lord and of Gideon!" and Midian melted away before them. So shall it be with our sins and doubts and fears, if we believe in Jesus, the incarnate God; they shall vanish like the mists of the morning. The Lord Jesus will break the yoke of our burden, and the rod of our oppressor, as in the day of Midian. Be of good courage, ye that are in bondage to fierce and cruel adversaries; for in the name of Jesus, who is God with us, you shall destroy them. This you see in the fourth verse. Please follow me as I dwell on each verse.

When Jesus comes, you shall have eternal peace; for His battle is the end of battles. "All the armor of the armed man in the tumult, and the garments rolled in blood, shall even be for burning, for fuel of fire." This is the rendering of the Revision; and it is good. The Prince of peace wars against war, and destroys it. What a glorious day is that in which the Lord breaks the bow and cuts the spear in sunder, and burns the chariot in the fire! I think I see it now. My sins, which were the weapons of my foes, the Lord piles in heaps. What mountains of prey! But see! He brings the firebrand of His love from the altar of His sacrifice, and He sets fire to the gigantic pile. See how they blaze! They are utterly consumed forever. The Enemy has now no weapon that he can use against my soul. The incarnate God has broken the power of the adversary, for the sting of death is sin, and that He has made an end of. He has thus destroyed the war which raged in our souls, and now He reigns as Prince of Peace, and we have peace in Him.

Now is it that the Lord Jesus becomes glorious in our eyes; and He whose name is Immanuel is now crowned in our hearts with many crowns, and honored with many titles. What a list of glories we have here! What a burst of song it makes when we sing of the Messiah: "His name shall be called Wonderful, Counselor, the Mighty God, the Everlasting Father, the Prince of Peace"! Each word sounds like a salvo of artillery. It is all very well to hear players on instruments and sweet singers rehearse these words; but to believe them, and realize them in your own soul, is better far. When every fear and every hope, and every power and every passion of our nature fill the orchestra of our hearts, and all unite in one inward song to the glorious Immanuel, what music it is! He is to us the Wonderful, the Counselor, the Mighty God, the Everlasting Father, the Prince of Peace, and much more than words can tell. Do but get Christ Jesus in your soul, as the incarnate God, and He will set up a government within your nature which shall bring you peace and righteousness and joy and eternal glory. He will so reign over you that your happiness shall know no bound; but you shall climb from grace to grace, from joy to joy, from peace to peace, yes, from heaven to the highest heaven. This all along shall be your divinest comfort, that Jesus is both God and man, even God with us.

Thus have I very briefly skimmed over the connection. Had we time and grace, what a wealth of thought might be drawn from these inexhaustible mines!

Certain Truths Connected with the Theme

But now, secondly, I want to press home certain truths connected with my theme. Come, Holy Spirit, to help the preacher! Come, divine Comforter, to troubled hearts, and give them rest in Immanuel!

Immanuel is a grand word. "God with us" means more than tongue can tell. It means enmity removed on our part, and justice vindicated on God's part. It means the whole Godhead engaged on our side, resolved to bless us.

But you say to me, "Who is this? Are you sure that Immanuel is Jesus of Nazareth?" Yes, *Jesus is Immanuel.* Will you turn to Matthew 1:21, and read onward, "And she shall bring forth a son, and thou shalt call his name JESUS: for he shall save his people from their sins. Now all this was done, that it might be fulfilled which was spoken of the Lord by the prophet, saying: Behold, a virgin shall be with child, and shall bring forth a son, and they shall call his name Emmanuel, which being interpreted is, God with us." Do you see this? They call His name Jesus to fulfill the prophecy that they should call His name Immanuel! It is a singular fulfillment surely. It can only be accounted for by the fact that the Holy Spirit regards the name "Jesus" as being tantamount to the name "Immanuel." The Savior is God with us. Jesus, a Savior, is, in the Hebrew, *Joshua,* or *Jehoshua,* that is, "Jehovah saving." The sense is the same as that of *Immanuel,* or "God with us," or for us; since God for us is sure to save us. The two names are the same in essential meaning. If

God has come to save, then God is with us; if God Himself is our salvation, then God is on our side; and if the child born of the virgin be indeed the Lord of glory, then is God our friend. Strong Son of God!
Immortal Love! We have not seen Your face; but we can trust Your
power, and rest upon Your love. Your very birth brings hope; but as for
Your death, when You bore our sins in Your own body on the tree, this is
the fulfillment of all our desires, in the canceling of sin, the removal of
wrath, and the securing of eternal life. Yes, Jesus is God with us.

Perhaps you wish to know a little more of the incident in the text
which exhibits *Jesus as the great light*. We have spoken of Zebulun and
Naphtali: were those regions really benefited by the coming of the Lord
Jesus? Just look a little further on to Matthew 4:12: "Now when Jesus
had heard that John was cast into prison, he departed into Galilee; And
leaving Nazareth, he came and dwelt in Capernaum, which is upon the
sea coast, in the borders of Zabulon and Nephthalim: That it might be
fulfilled which was spoken by Esaias the prophet, saying, The land of
Zabulon, and the land of Nephthalim, by the way of the sea, beyond
Jordan, Galilee of the Gentiles: The people which sat in darkness saw
great light; and to them which sat in the region and shadow of death
light is sprung up. From that time Jesus began to preach, and to say,
Repent: for the kingdom of heaven is at hand."

Yes, beloved, our Lord made His home in the darkest parts. He
looked about and saw no country so ignorant, no country so sorrowful,
as Galilee of the Gentiles, and therefore He went there, and lifted it up
to heaven by priceless privileges. His ministry of repentance and faith
was in itself a glorious light; but He did many mighty works to confirm
it. Why, the whole country around was full of sick folk whom He had
restored. You could not go half a mile but what you met a blind man
who told of how Jesus had restored his sight, or a sick woman who had
been raised up from the fever, or some paralytic who had been made
whole. That country must have been glad indeed. Multitudes would
never forget how they heard Him by the sea. They said, "What sermons
He preached! He made our hearts dance for joy; and then He fed us,
and we ate of barley loaves and little fish until we were filled. He is a
wonderful prophet, and this is a wonderful country; once dark enough,
but now enlightened by His presence." Beloved, I pray that Jesus may
come to you if you are in the dark today, and work miracles for you,
feed you, and teach you, and make you glad, so that, though you were
the most unhappy of beings, you may become the happiest of mortal
men. Galilee, plundered, despoiled, despised, became, by and by, glorious, because of Him who is Immanuel. This is a happy omen for you,
dear friends: if you have been the most sorrowful of beings, the Lord
Jesus may come at once to you and make you rejoice with great joy.

Jesus rescues from contempt, from ignorance, from misery, from despair, and therein reveals Himself as God with us.

We will turn back to where we opened our Bibles at the first, and there we learn that, to be God with us, *Jesus must be accepted by us.* He cannot be with us if we will not have Him. Hear how the prophet words it: "Unto us a child is born, unto us a son is given." As a child He was born, as a son He was given. He comes to us in two ways—in His human nature, born; in His divine nature, given. But I want you to see that all the sweetness and light that can come to you through Him must come by your putting both your hands upon Him, and taking Him to be your own. Here is one hand, *"Unto us* a child is born"; here is the other, *"Unto us* a son is given." Do you ask, "What are these two hands?"

I received a note from one of my hearers, who pleads, "Tell me, sir, what faith is; tell me what you mean by believing and trusting." My dear friend, I am always telling you that, and I mean to keep on always telling you it so long as I have a tongue to move. By a daring act of appropriation take Jesus to be yours, and say with me—oh, that we could all say it in one great shout!—*"Unto us a child is born, unto us a son is given."* God gives Him, we take Him. He is born, we take Him up in our arms, and feel ready to cry, "Lord, now lettest thou thy servant depart in peace; for mine eyes have seen thy salvation." He is a Son given. Shall we not accept this gift of gifts, and love Him because He has first loved us? To believe is to take freely what God gives freely. It is the simplest thing that can be. I could not explain to you what to drink is; but I will put this glass to my lips, and actually perform the action. Now you see what it is. The water is put to the lip, it is allowed to flow into the mouth and down the throat, and so it is drunk.

Take Christ just so. Up to the very lip of your reception He flows; open the mouth of your soul, and take Him into yourself. "May I?" say you. May you? You are threatened with damnation if you do not; for this is one side of the Gospel message, "He that believeth and is baptized shall be saved; he that believeth not shall be damned." A man may certainly do that which involves him in condemnation if he does not do it. That awful threatening is one of the most powerful bits of Gospel that I know of: it drives while the promise draws. If you want Christ, you may have Him. If you desire to have God with you, He waits to be gracious to you. If you wish for Immanuel, behold Him in Jesus, your Lord.

"Oh, but I wish I had some sign that I might be sure!" What sign do you want beyond the gift of God, the birth of Jesus? Away with demands which are wild and ungenerous. The Word of God bids you believe and live. The moment you believe in Jesus He is yours. Say, then, this morning, "Unto us a child is born, unto us a son is given," and say it with fullness of delight.

Be sure that you go on with the verse to the end—"and the government shall be upon his shoulder." If Christ is your Savior He must be your King.

> But know, nor of the terms complain,
> Where Jesus comes he comes to reign:
> To reign, and with no partial sway;
> Lusts must be slain that disobey.

The moment we really believe in Jesus as our salvation we fall before Him, and call Him Master and Lord. We serve when He saves. He has redeemed us to Himself, and we own that we are His. A generous man once bought a slave girl. She was put upon the block for auction, and he pitied her and purchased her; but when he had bought her he said to her, "I have bought you to set you free. There are your papers, you are a free woman." The grateful creature fell at his feet and cried, "I will never leave you; if you have made me free I will be your servant as long as you live, and serve you better than any slave could do."

This is how we feel toward Jesus. He sets us free from the dominion of Satan, and then, as we need a ruler, we say, "And the government shall be upon his shoulder." We are glad to be ruled by Immanuel, God with us. This also is a door of hope to us. That Jesus shall be the monarch of our hearts is our exceeding joy. To us He shall be always Wonderful. When we think of Him, or speak about Him, it shall be with reverent awe. When we need advice and comfort, we will fly to Him, for He shall be our Counselor. When we need strength, we will look to Him as our Mighty God. Born again by His Spirit, we will be His children, and He shall be the Everlasting Father. Full of joy and rest, we will call Him Prince of Peace.

Are you willing to have Christ to govern you? Will you spend your lives in praising Him? You are willing to have Christ to pardon you, but we cannot divide Him, and therefore you must also have Him to sanctify you. You must not take the crown from His head, but accept Him as the monarch of your soul. If you would have His hand to help you, you must obey the scepter which it grasps. Blessed Immanuel, we are right glad to obey You! In You our darkness ends, and from the shadow of death we rise to the light of life. It is salvation to be obedient to You. It is the end of gloom to her that was in anguish to bow herself before You. May God the Holy Spirit take of the things of Christ and show them to us, and then we shall all cry—

> Go worship at Immanuel's feet!
> See in his face what wonders meet!
> Faith is too narrow to express
> His worth, his grace, his righteousness.

2

The Sages, the Star, and the Savior

Where is he that is born King of the Jews? for we have seen his star in the east, and are come to worship him (Matthew 2:2).

The incarnation of the Son of God was one of the greatest events in the history of the universe. Its actual occurrence was not, however, known to all mankind, but was specially revealed to the shepherds of Bethlehem and to certain wise men of the east. To shepherds—the illiterate, men little versed in human learning—the angels in choral song made known the birth of the Savior, Christ the Lord, and they hastened to Bethlehem to see the great sight; the scribes, the writers of the law and expounders of it, knew nothing concerning the long-promised birth of the Messias. No angelic bands entered the assembly of the Sanhedrim and proclaimed that the Christ was born; and when the chief priests and Pharisees were met together, though they gathered around copies of the law to consider where Christ should be born, yet it was not known to them that He was actually come, nor do they seem to have taken more than a passing interest in the matter, though they might have known that then was the time spoken of by the prophets when the great Messiah should come. How mysterious are the dispensations of grace; the base things are chosen and the eminent are passed by! The advent of the Redeemer is revealed to the shepherds who kept their flocks of sheep by night, but not to the shepherds whose benighted sheep were left to stray. Admire therein the sovereignty of God.

The glad tidings were made known also to wise men, magi, students of the stars and of old prophetic books, from the far-off east. It would

---

This sermon was taken from *The Metropolitan Tabernacle Pulpit* and was preached on Sunday morning, December 25, 1870.

not be possible to tell how far off their native country lay; it may have been so distant that the journey occupied nearly the whole of the two years of which they spoke concerning the appearance of the star. Traveling was slow in those days, surrounded with difficulties and many dangers. They may have come from Persia, or India, or Tartary, or even from the mysterious land of Sinim, now known to us as China. If so, strange and uncouth must have been the speech of those who worshiped around the young child at Bethlehem, yet needed He no interpreter to understand and accept their adoration. Why was the birth of the King of the Jews made known to these foreigners, and not to those nearer home? Why did the Lord select those who were so many hundreds of miles away, while the children of the kingdom, in whose very midst the Savior was brought forth, were yet strangely ignorant of His presence? See here again another instance of the sovereignty of God.

Both in shepherds and in Eastern magi gathering around the young child, I see God dispensing His favors as He wills; and, as I see it, I exclaim, "I thank thee, O Father, Lord of heaven and earth, because thou hast hid these things from the wise and prudent, and hast revealed them unto babes. Even so, Father; for so it seemed good in thy sight." Herein we see again another instance of God's sovereign will; for as of old there were many widows in Israel in the days of Elias the prophet, but to none of them was Elias sent, save to the woman of Sarepta; so many there were who were called wise men among the Jews, but to none of them did the star appear; but it shone on Gentile eyes, and led a chosen company from the ends of the earth to bow at Emmanuel's feet.

Sovereignty in these cases clothed itself in the robes of mercy. It was great mercy that regarded the low estate of the shepherds, and it was far-reaching mercy which gathered from lands which lay in darkness a company of men made wise to salvation. Mercy wearing her resplendent jewels was present with divine sovereignty in the lowly abode of Bethlehem. Is it not a delightful thought that around the cradle of the Savior, as well as around His throne in the highest heaven, these two attributes meet? He makes known Himself—and herein is mercy; but it is to those whom He has chosen—and herein He shows that He will have mercy on whom He will have mercy, and He will have compassion on whom He will have compassion.

We will now endeavor to learn a practical lesson from the story of the wise men who came from the east to worship Christ. We may, if God the Holy Spirit shall teach us, gather such instruction as may lead us also to become worshipers of the Savior, and joyful believers in Him.

Notice, first, *their inquiry*; may many of us become inquirers upon the same matter—"Where is he that is born King of the Jews?" Notice, secondly, *their encouragement*—"We have seen his star." Because they had seen His star they felt bold to ask, "Where is he?" And then, thirdly, *their example*—"We have come to worship him."

Their Inquiry—"Where is he?"

Many things are evident in this question. It is clear that when the wise men thus inquired, there was in their minds *interest awakened.* The King of the Jews was born, but Herod did not ask: "Where is he?" until his jealousy was excited, and then he asked the question in a malicious spirit. Christ was born at Bethlehem, near to Jerusalem; yet throughout all the streets of the holy city there were no inquirers, "Where is he?" He was to be the glory of Israel, and yet in Israel there were few indeed who, like these wise men, asked the question, "Where is he?"

My dear hearers, I will believe that there are some here this morning whom God intends to bless, and it will be a very hopeful sign that He intends to do so if there be an interest awakened in your mind concerning the work and person of the incarnate God. Those who anxiously desire to know of Him, are but a slender company. Alas! when we preach most earnestly of Him and tell of His sorrows as the atonement for human sin, we are compelled to lament most bitterly the carelessness of mankind, and inquire mournfully

> Is it nothing to you, all ye that pass by;
> Is it nothing to you that Jesus should die?

He is despised and rejected of men, men see in Him no beauty that they should desire Him; but there are a chosen number who inquire diligently, and who come to receive Him; to these He gives power to become the sons of God. A happy circumstance it is, therefore, when there is interest evinced.

Interest is not always evinced in the things of Christ, even by our regular hearers. It gets to be a mere mechanical habit to attend public worship; you become accustomed to sit through such a part of the service, to stand and sing at such another time, and to listen to the preacher with an apparent attention during the discourse; but to be really interested, to long to know what it is all about, to know especially whether you have a part in it, whether Jesus came from heaven to save you, whether for you He was born of the virgin, to make such personal inquiries with deep anxiety, is far from being a general practice: would God that all who have ears to hear would hear in truth. Wherever the word is heard with solemn interest, it is a very encouraging sign. It was said of old, "They shall ask the way to Zion with their faces thitherward." When a man listens with deep attention to the Word of God, searches God's Book, and engages in thoughtful meditation with the view of understanding the Gospel, we have much hope of him. When he feels that there is something weighty and important, something worth the knowing, in the Gospel of Jesus, then are we encouraged to hope good things of him.

But in the case of the wise men we see not only interest evinced, but *belief avowed.* They said, "Where is he that is born King of the Jews?" They were, therefore, fully convinced that He was the King of the Jews, and had lately been born.

As a preacher I feel it to be a great mercy that I have to deal generally with persons who have some degree of belief concerning the things of God. Would to God we had more missions to those who have no sort of faith and no knowledge of Christ; and may the day come when everywhere Jesus Christ shall be known. But here at home with the most of you we have something to begin with. You do believe somewhat concerning Jesus of Nazareth, who was born King of the Jews. Set much store by that which you have already believed.

I count it no small advantage to a young man to believe his Bible true. There are some who have a hard fight to reach so far as that, for infidel training has warped their minds. It is not, of course, an advantage which will save you, for many go down to hell believing the Scriptures to be true, and thus they accumulate guilt upon themselves from that very fact; but it is a fine vantage ground to occupy, to be assured that you have God's Word before you, and not to be troubled with questions about its inspiration and authenticity. O that you may go from that point of faith to another, and become a hearty believer in Jesus.

These wise men were so far advanced that they had some leverage for a further lift of faith, for they believed that Christ was born, and born a King. Many who are not saved yet know that Jesus is the Son of God. We have not to argue with you this morning to bring you out of Socinianism—no, you believe Jesus to be the divine Savior; nor have we to reason against doubts and skepticisms concerning the atonement, for these do not perplex you. This is a great mercy.

You certainly stand in the position of highly favored persons. I only trust you may have grace given you to avail yourselves of the favorable position in which God has placed you. Value what you have already received. When a man's eyes have long been closed in darkness, if the oculist gives him but a little light he is very thankful for it, he is hopeful that the eye is not destroyed, that perhaps by another operation further scales may be removed, and the full light may yet stream in upon the darkened eyeball. So, dear friend, be thankful for any light. O soul, so soon to pass into another world, so sure to be lost except you have the light divine, so certain to be cast into the outer darkness, where there is weeping and wailing and gnashing of teeth, be thankful for a spark of heavenly light; prize it, treasure it, be anxious about it that it may come to something more, and who knows but yet the Lord will bless you with the fullness of His truth?

When the great bridge across the Niagara was made, the difficulty was to pass the first rope across the broad stream. I have read that it was accomplished by flying a kite, and allowing it to fall on the opposite bank. The kite carried across a piece of string, then to the string was tied a line, and to the line a rope, and to the rope a stronger rope, and by and by Niagara was spanned, and the bridge was finished. Even thus by degrees God works. It is a fair sight to see in human hearts a little interest concerning things divine, a little desire after Christ, a feeble wish to know who He is and what He is, and whether He is available to the sinner's case. This hunger will lead to a craving after more, and that craving will be followed by another, until at last the soul shall find her Lord and be satisfied in Him. In the wise men's case therefore we have, as I trust we have in some here, interest evinced, and a measure of belief avowed.

Furthermore, in the case of the wise men, we see *ignorance admitted*. Wise men are never above asking questions, because they are wise men; so the magi asked, "Where is he?" Persons who have taken the name and degree of wise men, and are so esteemed, sometimes think it beneath them to confess any degree of ignorance, but the really wise think not so; they are too well instructed to be ignorant of their own ignorance. Many men might have been wise if they had but been aware that they were fools.

The knowledge of our ignorance is the doorstep of the temple of knowledge. Some think they know, and therefore never know. Had they known that they were blind, they would soon have been made to see, but because they say, "We see," therefore their blindness remains upon them.

Beloved hearer, do you want to find a Savior? Would you fain have all your sins blotted out? Would you be reconciled to God through Jesus Christ? Then blush not to inquire, admit that you do not know. How should you know if heaven teach you not? How should any man attain the knowledge of divine things, unless it be given him from above? We must all be taught of the Spirit of God, or be fools forever. To know that we need to be taught of the Holy Spirit is one of the first lessons that the Holy Spirit Himself teaches us. Admit that you need a guide, and diligently inquire for one. Cry to God to lead you, and He will be your instructor. Be not high-minded and self-sufficient. Ask for heavenly light, and you shall receive it. Is it not better to ask God to teach you, than to trust to your own unaided reason? Bow, then, the knee, confess your aptness to err, and say, "What I know not, teach me."

Notice, however, that the wise men were not content with admitting their ignorance, but in their case there was *information entreated*. I cannot tell where they began to ask. They thought it likeliest that Jesus would be known at the metropolitan city. Was He not the King of the Jews? where would He be so certain to be known as at the capital? They went, therefore, to Jerusalem. Perhaps they asked the guards at the gate, "Where is he that is born King of the Jews?" and the guards laughed them to scorn, and replied, "We know no king but Herod." Then they met a loiterer in the streets, and to him they said, "Where is he that is born King of the Jews?" and he answered, "What care I for such crazy questions? I am looking for a drinking companion." They asked a trader, but he sneered, and said, "Never mind kings, what will you buy, or what have you to sell?" "Where is he that is born King of the Jews?" said they to a Sadducee, and he replied, "Be not such fools as to talk in that fashion, or if you do, pray call on my religious friend the Pharisee." They passed a woman in the streets, and asked, "Where is he that is born King of the Jews?" but she said, "My child is sick at home, I have enough to do to think of my poor babe; I care not who is born, or who may die beside." When they went to the very highest quarters, they obtained but poor information, but they were not content until they had learned all that could be known. They did not know at first where the newborn King was, but they used every means to find Him, and asked information on all hands.

It is delightful to see the holy eagerness of a soul which God has quickened; it cries, "I must be saved; I know something of the way of salvation, I am grateful for that, but I do not know all I want to know, and I cannot rest satisfied until I do. If beneath the canopy of heaven a Savior is to be found, I will have Him; if that book can teach me how to be saved, I will turn its pages day and night; if any book within my reach may help me, I will spare no midnight oil if I may but in the reading thereof find out Christ my Savior. If there be one whose preaching has been blessed to the souls of others, I will hang on his lips, if perhaps the word may be blessed to me, for Christ I must have. It is not I may or I may not have Him, but I *must* have Him; my hunger is great for this bread of heaven, my thirst insatiable for this water of life. Tell me, Christians, tell me, wise men, tell me, good men, tell me any of you who can tell, where is He that is born King of the Jews? For Christ I must have, and I long to have Him now."

Notice further, that in reference to these wise men from the east, there was for their search after Christ *a motive declared*. "Where is he," said they, "that we may go and worship him?" Ah! soul, and if you would find Christ, let it be your motive that you may be saved by Him, and that then henceforth and forever you may live to His glory. When it comes to this, that you do not hear the Gospel merely as a habit, but because you long to obtain its salvation, it will not be long before you will find it. When a man can say, "I am going up to the house of God this morning, and O may God meet with me there," he will not long go there in vain. When a hearer can declare, "As soon as I take my seat in the congregation, my one thought is, "Lord, bless my soul this day!" he cannot for long be disappointed. Usually in going up to God's house we get what we go for. Some come because it is the custom, some to meet a friend, some they scarce know why; but when you know what you come for, the Lord who gave you the desire will gratify it.

I was pleased with the word of a dear sister this morning when I came in at the back gate; she said to me, "My dear sir, my soul is very hungry this morning. May the Lord give you bread for me." I believe that food convenient will be given. When a sinner is very hungry after Christ, Christ is very near to him. The worst of it is, many of you do not come to find Jesus, it is not Him you are seeking for; if you were seeking Him, He would soon appear to you.

A young woman was asked during a revival, "How is it you have not found Christ?" "Sir," said she, "I think it is because I have not sought Him." It is so. None shall be able to say at the last, "I sought Him, but I found Him not." In all cases at the last, if Jesus Christ be not found, it must be because He has not been devoutly, earnestly, importunately sought, for His promise is, "Seek, and ye shall find." These wise men are to us a model in many things, and in this among the rest—that their motive was clear to themselves, and they avowed it to others. May all of us seek Jesus that we may worship Him.

All through there was about the wise men an intense earnestness which we would delight to see in any who as yet have not believed in Jesus. They were evidently not triflers. They came a long way, they underwent many fatigues, they spoke about finding the newborn King in a practical, commonsense way; they were not put off with this rebuff or that; they desired to find Him, and find Him they would. It is most blessed to see the work of the Spirit in men's hearts impelling them to long for the Savior to be their Lord and King, and so to long for Him that they mean to have Him, and will leave no stone unturned, by the Holy Spirit's help, but what they will be able to say, "We have found him, of whom Moses in the law, and the prophets, did write," and "He is become our salvation."

Am I at this moment speaking to anybody in particular? I trust I am. Some years ago there was a young man, who, upon much such a morning as this—cold, snowy, dark—entered a house of prayer, as you have done today. I thought as I came here this morning of that young man. I said to myself, "This morning is so very forbidding that I shall have a very small congregation, but perhaps among them there will be one like that young man." To be plain with you, it comforted me to think that the morning when God blessed my soul, the preacher had a very small congregation, and it was cold and bitter, and therefore I said to myself this morning, "Why should not I go up merrily to my task, and preach if there should only be a dozen there?" for Jesus may intend to reveal Himself to someone as He did to me, and that someone may be a soul-winner, and the means of the salvation of tens of thousands in years to come. I wonder if that will occur to that young man yonder, for I trust he has the inquiry of the wise men upon his lips. I trust he will not quench those desires which now burn within him, but rather may the spark be fanned to a flame, and may this day witness his decision for Jesus. Oh, has the Lord looked on that young woman, or on that dear child, or on yonder aged man? I know not who it may be, but I shall indeed bless God this morning, if the cry may be heard from many a lip, "Sir, what must I do to be saved? Where is he that is born King of the Jews?"

Their Encouragement—"We have seen his star."

Having spoken of their inquiry, I shall now notice their encouragement. Something encouraged these wise men to seek Jesus. It was this, "We have seen his star."

Now, the most of you seekers after Christ have a great encouragement in the fact that you have heard His Gospel; you live in a land where you have the Scriptures, where the ordinances of God's house are freely dispensed. These are, as it were, Jesus Christ's star; they are meant to lead you to Him. Here observe, that to see His star was a great favor. It was not given to all the dwellers in the east or west to see His star. These men, therefore, were highly privileged. It is not given to all mankind to hear the Gospel, Jesus is not preached in all our streets; His Cross is not lifted high even in every place that is dedicated to His worship. You are highly favored, O my friend, it you have seen the star, the Gospel, which points to Jesus.

To see the star involved these wise men in *great responsibility*. For, suppose they had seen His star and had not set out to worship Him, they would have been far more guilty than others, who, not having received such an indication from heaven, would not have been able to set it at nothing. Oh, think of the responsibility of some of you, who in your childhood heard of a Savior, for whom a mother has wept many tears; you know the truth, in the theory of it at any rate; you have the responsibility of having seen His star.

The wise men *did not regard the favor of seeing the star as a matter to be rested in.* They did not say, "We have seen His star, and that is enough." Many say, "Well, we attend a place of worship regularly, is not that enough?" There are those who say, "We were baptized, baptism brought regeneration with it; we come to the sacrament, and do we not get grace through it?" Poor souls! the star which leads to Christ they mistake for Christ Himself, and worship the star instead of the Lord. O may none of you ever be so foolish as to rest in outward ordinances!

God will say to you, if you depend upon sacraments or upon public worship, "Bring no more vain oblations; incense is an abomination unto me. Who hath required this at your hands, to tread my courts?" What cares God for outward forms and ceremonies? When I see men putting on white gowns, and scarves and bands, and singing their prayers, and bowing and scraping, I wonder what sort of god it is they worship. Surely he must have more affinity with the gods of the heathen than with the great Jehovah who has made the heavens and the earth.

Mark well the exceeding glory of Jehovah's works on sea and land; behold the heavens and their countless hosts of stars, hark to the howling of the winds and the rush of the hurricane, think of Him who makes the clouds His chariot, and rides on the wings of the wind, and then consider whether this infinite God is like to that being to whom it is a matter of grave consequence whether a cup of wine is lifted in worship as high as a man's hair or only as high as his nose!

O foolish generation, to think that Jehovah is contained in your temples made with hands, and that He cares for your vestments, your processions, your postures, and your genuflections. You fight over your ritual, even to its jots and tittles do you consider it. Surely you know not the glorious Jehovah, if you conceive that these things yield any pleasure to Him. Nay, beloved, we desire to worship the Most High in all simplicity and earnestness of spirit, and never to stop in the outward form, lest we be foolish enough to think that to see the star is sufficient, and therefore fail to find the incarnate God.

Note well, that these wise men *did not find satisfaction in what they had themselves done to reach the child.* As we have observed, they may have come hundreds of miles, but they did not mention it; they did not sit down and say, "Well, we have journeyed across deserts, over hills, and across rivers, it is enough." No, they must find the newborn King, nothing else would satisfy them. Do not say, dear hearer, "I have been praying now for months, I have been searching the Scriptures for weeks, to find the Savior." I am glad you have done so, but do not rest in it; you must get Christ, or else you perish after all your exertion and your trouble. Jesus you want, nothing more than Jesus, but nothing less than Jesus. Nor must you be satisfied with traveling in the way the star would lead you, you must reach HIM. Do not stop short of eternal life. Lay hold on it, not merely seek it and long for it, but lay hold on eternal life, and do not be content until it is an ascertained fact with you that Jesus Christ is yours.

I should like you to notice how these wise men were not satisfied with merely getting to Jerusalem. They might have said, "Ah! now we are in the land where the child is born, we will be thankful and sit down." No, but "Where is he?" He is born at Bethlehem. Well, they get to Bethlehem, but we do not find that when they reached that village they said, "This is a favored spot, we will sit down here." Not at all, they wanted to know where the house was. They reached the house, and the star got over it. It was a fair sight to see the cottage with the star above it, and to think that the newborn King was there, but that did not satisfy them. No, they went right into the house; they rested not until they saw the child Himself and had worshiped Him.

I pray that you and I may always be so led by the Spirit of God that we may never put up with anything short of a real grasping of Christ, a believing sight of Christ as a Savior, as our Savior, as our Savior even now. If there be one danger above another that the young seeker should strive against, it is the danger of stopping short of a hearty faith in Jesus Christ. While your heart is tender like wax, take care that no seal but the seal of Christ be set on you. Now that you are uneasy and out of comfort, make this your vow, "I will not be comforted until Jesus comfort me." It would be better for you never to be awakened than to be lulled to sleep by Satan—for a sleep that follows upon a partial conviction is generally a deeper slumber than any other that falls upon the sons of men. My soul, I charge you get to the blood of Christ, and be washed in it; get to the life of Christ, and let that life be in you, that you be indeed God's child; put not up with suppositions, be not satisfied with appearances and perhapses; rest nowhere until you have said— God having given you the faith to say it, "He loved me and gave Himself for me, He is all my salvation and all my desire."

See, then, how these wise men were not made by the sight of the star to keep away from Christ, but they were encouraged by it to come to Christ, and do you be encouraged, dear seeker, this morning to come to Jesus by the fact that you are blessed with the Gospel. You have an invitation given you to come to Jesus, you have the motions of God's Spirit upon your conscience, awakening you; O come, come and welcome, and let this strange winter's day be a day of brightness and of gladness to a many a seeking soul.

I have turned my thoughts on this last head into verse, and I will repeat the lines—

O where is Christ my King?
I languish for the sight,
Fain would I fall to worshiping,
For he's my soul's delight.

Himself, himself alone,
I seek no less, no more,
Or on his cross, or on his throne,
I'd equally adore.

The sages saw his star,
But rested not content,
The way was rough, the distance far,
Yet on that way they went,

And now my thoughts discern
The sign that Christ is nigh,
With love unquenchable I burn,
T' enjoy his company.

No star nor heavenly sign
My soul's desire can fill,
For him, my Lord, my King divine,
My soul is thirsting still.

The Example

And now we shall conclude, by considering the example of these wise men. They came to Jesus, and in so doing, they did three things: they saw, they worshiped, they gave. Those are three things which every believer here may do this morning over again, and which every seeker should do for the first time.

First, *they saw* the young child. I do not think they merely said, "There He is," and so ended the matter, but they stood still and looked. Perhaps for some minutes they did not speak. About His very face I do not doubt there was a supernatural beauty. Whether there was a beauty to everyone's eye I know not, but to theirs there was assuredly a super-human attraction. The incarnate God! They gazed with their eyes. They looked, and looked, and looked again. They glanced at His mother, but they fixed their eyes on Him. "They saw the young child."

So, too, this morning let us think of Jesus with fixed and continuous thought. He is God, He is man, He is the substitute for sinners; He is willing to receive all who trust Him. He will save, and save this morning, every one of us who will rely upon Him. Think of Him. If you are at home this afternoon, spend the time in thinking upon Him. Bring Him before your mind's eye, consider and admire Him. Is it not a wonder that God should enter into union with man and come to this world as an infant? He who made heaven and earth hangs on a woman's breast for us! For our redemption the Word was made flesh.

This truth will breed the brightest hope within your soul. If you follow that babe's wondrous life until it ends at the Cross, I trust you may there be able to give such a look at Him that, like as Moses lifted up the serpent in the wilderness, and they that looked were healed, so you looking may be healed of all your spiritual diseases. Though it is many a year since I first looked to Him, I desire to look to Jesus again. The incarnate God! My eyes swim with tears to think that He who might have crushed me into hell forever becomes a young child for my sake! See Him, all of you, and seeing worship.

What did the wise men next? They *worshiped* Him. We cannot properly worship a Christ whom we do not know. "To the unknown God" is poor worship. But, oh, when you think of Jesus Christ, whose goings forth were of old from everlasting, the eternally begotten Son of the Father, and then see Him coming here to be a man of the substance of His mother, and know and understand why He came and what He did when He came, then you fall down and worship Him.

> Son of God, to thee we bow,
> Thou art Lord, and only thou;
> Thou the woman's promised seed;
> Thou who didst for sinners bleed.

We worship Jesus. Our faith sees Him go from the manger to the Cross, and from the Cross right up to the throne, and there where Jehovah dwells, amidst the insufferable glory of the divine presence stands the man, the very man who slept at Bethlehem in the manger; there He reigns as Lord of Lords. Our souls worship Him again. You are our Prophet, every word You say, Jesu, we believe and desire to follow. You are our Priest, Your sacrifice has made us clean, we are washed in Your blood; You are our King, command, we will obey, lead on, and we will follow. We worship You. We should spend much time in worshiping the Christ, and He should ever have the highest place in our reverence.

After worshiping, the wise men presented *their gifts*. One broke open his casket of gold and laid it at the feet of the newborn King. Another presented frankincense—one of the precious products of the country from which they came; and others laid myrrh at the Redeemer's feet; all these they gave to prove the truth of their worship. They gave substantial offerings with no niggard hand. And now, after you have worshiped Christ in your soul, and seen Him with the eye of faith, it will not need that I should say to you, give Him yourself, give

Him your heart, give Him your substance. Why, you will not be able to help doing it. He who really loves the Savior in his heart cannot help devoting to Him his life, his strength, his all. With some people, when they give Christ anything or do anything for Him, it is dreadfully forced work. They say, "The love of Christ ought to constrain us." I do not know that there is any such text as that in the Bible, however. I do remember one text that runs thus—"The love of Christ constraineth us." If it does not constrain us, it is because it is not in us. It is not merely a thing which ought to be, it must be. If any man love Christ, he will very soon be finding out ways and means of proving his love by his sacrifices. Go home, Mary, and fetch the alabaster box, and pour the ointment on His head, and if any say, "Wherefore is this waste?" you will have a good reply, you have had much forgiven you, and therefore you love much. If you have gold, give it; if you have frankincense, give it; if you have myrrh, give it to Jesus; and if you have none of these things, give Him your love, all your love, and that will be gold and spices all in one; give Him your tongue, speak of Him; give Him your hands, work for Him; give Him your whole self. I know you will, for He loved you, and gave Himself for you. The Lord bless you, and may this Christmas Sabbath morning be a very memorable day to many out of the crowd assembled here. I am surprised to see so vast a number present, and I can only hope the blessing will be in proportion, for Jesus' sake. Amen.

3

The Incarnation and Birth of Christ

But thou, Bethlehem Ephratah, though thou be little among the thousands of Judah, yet out of thee shall he come forth unto me that is to be ruler in Israel; whose goings forth have been from of old, from everlasting (Micah 5:2).

This is the season of the year when, whether we wish it or not, we are compelled to think of the birth of Christ. I hold it to be one of the greatest absurdities under heaven to think that there is any religion in keeping Christmas Day. There are no probabilities whatever that our Savior Jesus Christ was born on that day, and the observance of it is purely of popish origin; doubtless those who are Catholics have a right to hallow it, but I do not see how consistent Protestants can account it in the least sacred. However, I wish there were ten or a dozen Christmas Days in the year; for there is work enough in the world, and a little more rest would not hurt laboring people. Christmas Day is really a boon to us, particularly as it enables us to assemble around the family hearth and meet our friends once more. Still, although we do not fall exactly in the track of other people, I see no harm in thinking of the incarnation and birth of the Lord Jesus. We do not wish to be classed with those

> Who with more care keep holiday
> The wrong, than others the right way.

The old Puritans made a parade of work on Christmas Day, just to show that they protested against the observance of it. But we believe they entered that protest so completely, that we are willing, as their

---

This sermon was taken from *The New Park Street Pulpit* and was preached on Sunday morning, December 23, 1855.

31

descendants, to take the good accidentally conferred by the day, and leave its superstitions to the superstitious.

To proceed at once to what we have to say to you: we notice, first, *who it was that sent Christ forth.* God the Father here speaks, and says, "Out of thee shall he come forth unto *me* that is to be the ruler in Israel." Secondly, *where did He come to at the time of His incarnation?* Thirdly, *what did He come for?* "To be ruler in Israel." Fourthly, *had He ever come before?* Yes, He had. "Whose goings forth have been from of old, from everlasting."

Who Sent Jesus Christ?

Who sent Christ? The answer is returned to us by the words of the text. "Out of thee," says Jehovah, speaking by the mouth of Micah, "out of thee shall he come forth unto *me*." It is a sweet thought that Jesus Christ did not come forth without His Father's permission, authority, consent, and assistance. He was sent of the Father, that He might be the Savior of men. We are, alas! too apt to forget, that while there are distinctions as to persons in the Trinity there are no distinctions of honor; and we do very frequently ascribe the honor of our salvation, or at least the depths of its mercy and the extremity of its benevolence, more to Jesus Christ than we do to the Father. This is a very great mistake.

What if Jesus came? Did not His Father send Him? If He was made a child did not the Holy Spirit beget Him? If He spoke wondrously, did not His Father pour grace into His lips, that He might be an able minister of the new covenant? If His Father did forsake Him when He drank the bitter cup of gall, did He not love Him still? And did He not, by and by, after three days, raise Him from the dead, and at last receive Him up on high, leading captivity captive?

Ah! beloved, he who knows the Father, and the Son, and the Holy Spirit as he should know them, never sets one before another; he is not more thankful to one than the other; he sees them at Bethlehem, at Gethsemane, and on Calvary, all equally engaged in the work of salvation. "He shall come forth unto *me*."

O Christian, have you put your confidence in the man Christ Jesus? Have you placed your reliance solely on Him? And are you united with Him? Then believe that you are united to the God of heaven; since to the man Christ Jesus you are brother, and hold closest fellowship, you are linked thereby with God the Eternal, and "the Ancient of Days" is your Father and your friend. "He shall come forth unto *me*."

Did you never see the depth of love there was in the heart of Jehovah, when God the Father equipped His Son for the great enterprise of mercy? There had been a sad day in heaven once before, when

Satan fell, and dragged with him a third of the stars of heaven, and when the Son of God launching from His great right hand the Omnipotent thunders, dashed the rebellious crew to the pit of perdition; but if we could conceive a grief in heaven, that must have been a sadder day, when the Son of the Most High left His Father's bosom, where He had lain from before all worlds.

"Go," says the Father, "and Thy Father's blessing on Thy head!" Then comes the unrobing. How do angels crowd around to see the Son of God take off His robes! He laid aside His crown; He said, "My father, I am Lord over all, blessed forever, but I will lay My crown aside, and be as mortal men are." He strips Himself of His bright vest of glory; "Father," He says, "I will wear a robe of clay, just such as men wear." Then He takes off all those jewels wherewith He was glorified; He lays aside His starry mantles and robes of light, to dress Himself in the simple garments of the peasant of Galilee. What a solemn disrobing that must have been! And next, can you picture the dismissal! The angels attend the Savior through the streets, until they approach the doors: when an angel cries, "Lift up your heads, O ye gates, and be ye lifted up ye everlasting doors, and let the King of Glory through!" Oh! I think the angels must have wept when they lost the company of Jesus—when the Sun of heaven bereaved them of all its light. But they went after Him. They descended with Him; and when His spirit entered into flesh, and He became a babe, He was attended by that mighty host of angels, who after they had been with Him to Bethlehem's manger, and seen Him safely laid on His mother's breast, in their journey upward appeared to the shepherds and told them that He was born king of the Jews. *The Father* sent Him! Contemplate that subject. Let your soul get hold of it, and in every period of His life think that He suffered what *the Father* willed; that every step of His life was marked with the approval of the great I AM. Let every thought that you have of Jesus be also connected with the eternal, ever-blessed God; for "he," says Jehovah, "shall come forth unto *me*." Who sent Him, then? The answer is, His Father.

Where Did He Come To?

Where did He come? A word or two concerning Bethlehem. It seemed meet and right that our Savior should be born in Bethlehem, and that because of Bethlehem's history, Bethlehem's name, and Bethlehem's position—little in Judah.

First, it seemed necessary that Christ should be born in Bethlehem, *because of Bethlehem's history*. Dear to every Israelite was the little village of Bethlehem. Jerusalem might outshine it in splendor, for there stood the temple, the glory of the whole earth, and "beautiful for situation, the joy of the whole earth was Mount Zion"; yet around Bethlehem there clustered a number of incidents which always made it a pleasant resting place to every Jewish mind; and even the Christian cannot help loving Bethlehem. The first mention, I think, that we have of Bethlehem is a sorrowful one. There Rachel died. If you turn to the chapter thirty-five of Genesis you will find it said in the sixteenth verse:

"And they journeyed from Bethel; and there was but a little way to come to Ephrath; and Rachel travailed, and she had hard labor. And it came to pass, when she was in hard labor, that the midwife said unto her, Fear not; thou shalt have this son also. And it came to pass, as her soul was in departing, (for she died) that she called his name Ben-oni: but his father called him Benjamin. And Rachel died, and was buried in the way to Ephrath, which is Bethlehem. And Jacob set a pillar upon her grave, that is the pillar of Rachel's grave unto this day."

A singular incident this—almost prophetic. Might not Mary have called her own son Jesus, her Ben-oni; for He was to be the child of sorrow? Simeon said to her—"Yea, a sword shall pierce through thine own soul also, that the thoughts of many hearts may be revealed." But while she might have called Him Ben-oni, what did God His Father call Him? Benjamin, the son of My right hand. Ben-oni was He as a man; Benjamin as to His Godhead. This little incident seems to be almost a prophecy that Ben-oni—Benjamin, the Lord Jesus, should be born in Bethlehem.

But another woman makes this place celebrated. That woman's name was Naomi. There lived at Bethlehem in after days, when, perhaps, the stone that Jacob's fondness had raised had been covered with moss and its inscription obliterated, another woman, named Naomi. She too was a daughter of joy, and yet a daughter of bitterness. Naomi was a woman whom the Lord had loved and blessed, but she had to go to a strange land and she said, "Call me not Naomi (pleasant) but let my name be called Mara (bitter) for the Almighty hath dealt very bitterly with me."

Yet was she not alone amid all her losses, for there cleaved to her Ruth the Moabitess, whose Gentile blood should unite with the pure untainted stream of the Jew, and should thus bring forth the Lord our Savior, the great King both of Jews and Gentiles. That very beautiful book of Ruth had all its scenery laid in Bethlehem. It was at Bethlehem that Ruth went forth to glean in the fields of Boaz; it was there that Boaz looked upon her, and she bowed herself before her lord; it was there her marriage was celebrated; and in the streets of Bethlehem did Boaz and Ruth receive a blessing which made them fruitful, so that Boaz became the father of Obed, and Obed the father of Jesse, and Jesse the father of David.

That last fact gilds Bethlehem with glory—the fact that David was born there, the mighty hero who smote the Philistine giant, who led the discontented of his land away from the tyranny of their monarch, and who afterward, by a full consent of a willing people, was crowned king of Israel and Judah. Bethlehem was a royal city because the kings were there brought forth. Little as Bethlehem was, it was much to be esteemed; because it was like certain principalities which we have in Europe, which are celebrated for nothing but for bringing forth the consorts of the royal families of England. It was right, then, from history that Bethlehem should be the birthplace of Christ.

But again: *there is something in the name of the place.* "Bethlehem Ephratah." The word *Bethlehem* has a double meaning. It signifies "the house of bread," and "the house of war." Ought not Jesus Christ to be born in "the house of bread"? He is the Bread of His people, on which they feed. As our fathers ate manna in the wilderness, so do we live on Jesus here below. Famished by the world, we cannot feed on its shadows. Its husks may gratify the swinish taste of worldlings, for they are swine; but we need something more substantial, and in that blessed bread of heaven, made of the bruised body of our Lord Jesus, and baked in the furnace of His agonies, we find a blessed food. No food like Jesus to the desponding soul or to the strongest saint. The very meanest of the family of God goes to Bethlehem for his bread; and the strongest man, who eats strong meat, goes to Bethlehem for it.

House of Bread! whence could come our nourishment but from you? We have tried Sinai, but on her rugged steeps there grow no fruits, and her thorny heights yield no corn whereon we may feed. We have repaired even to Tabor itself, where Christ was transfigured, and yet there we have not been able to eat His flesh and drink His blood. But Bethlehem, you house of bread, rightly were you called; for there the bread of life was first handed down for man to eat.

And it is also called "the house of war"; because Christ is to a man "the house of bread," or else "the house of war." While He is food to the righteous He causes war to the wicked, according to His own word—"Think not that I am come to send peace on the earth; I am not come to send peace, but a sword. For I am come to set a man at variance against his father, and the daughter against her mother, and the daughter-in-law against her mother-in-law. And a man's foes shall be they of his own household."

Sinner! if you do not know Bethlehem as "the house of bread," it shall be to you a "house of war." If from the lips of Jesus you never drink sweet honey—if you are not like the bee, which sips sweet luscious liquor from the Rose of Sharon, then out of the selfsame mouth there shall go forth against you a two-edged sword; and that mouth from which the righteous draw their bread, shall be to you the mouth of destruction and the cause of your ill. Jesus of Bethlehem, house of bread and house of war, we trust we know You as our bread. Oh! that some who are now at war with You might hear in their hearts, as well as in their ears the song.—

> Peace on earth, and mercy mild,
> God and sinners reconciled.

And now for that word *Ephratah*. That was the old name of the place which the Jews retained and loved. The meaning of it is, "fruitfulness," or "abundance." Ah! well was Jesus born in the house of fruitfulness; for whence comes my fruitfulness and your fruitfulness, my brother, but from Bethlehem? Our poor barren hearts never produced one fruit, or flower, until they were watered with the Savior's blood. It is His incarnation which fattens the soil of our hearts. There had been pricking thorns on all the ground, and mortal poisons, before He came; but our fruitfulness comes from Him. "I am like a green fir-tree; from thee is my fruit found." "All my springs are in thee." If we be like trees planted by the rivers of water, bringing forth our fruit in our season, it is not because we were naturally fruitful, but because of the rivers of water by which we were planted. It is Jesus that makes us fruitful. "If a man abide in me," He says, "and my words abide in him, he shall bring forth much fruit." Glorious Bethlehem Ephratah! Rightly named! Fruitful house of bread—the house of abundant provision for the people of God!

We notice, next, *the position of Bethlehem*. It is said to be "little among the thousands of Judah." Why is this? Because Jesus Christ always goes among little ones. He was born in the little one among the thousands of Judah. Not Bashan's high hill, not on Hebron's royal mount, not in Jerusalem's palaces, but in the humble, yet illustrious, village of Bethlehem. There is a passage in Zechariah which teaches us a lesson—It is said that the man on the red horse stood among the myrtle trees. Now the myrtle trees grow at the bottom of the hill; and the man on the red horse always rides there. He does not ride on mountaintop; he rides among the humble in heart. "With this man will dwell, saith the Lord, with him who is of a humble and contrite spirit, and who trembleth at my word."

There are some little ones here this morning—"little among the thousands of Judah." No one ever heard your name, did were buried and had your name on your tombstone, it would noticed. Those who pass by would say, "It is nothing to me; I knew him." You do not know much of yourself, or think much of yourself; you can scarcely read, perhaps. Or if you have some talents and ability, you are despised among men; or, if you are not despised by them, you despise yourself. You are one of the little ones. Well, Christ is always born in Bethlehem among the little ones. Big hearts never get Christ inside of them; Christ lies not in great hearts, but in little ones. Mighty and proud spirits never have Jesus Christ, for He comes in at low doors, but He will not come in at high ones. He who has a broken heart and a low spirit shall have the Savior, but none else. He heals not the prince and the king, but "the broken in heart, and he bindeth up their wounds." Sweet thought! He is the Christ of the little ones. "Thou, Bethlehem Ephratah, though thou be little among the thousands of Judah, yet out of thee shall he come forth unto me that is to be ruler in Israel."

We cannot pass away from this without another thought here, which is, *how wonderfully mysterious was that providence which brought Jesus Christ's mother to Bethlehem at the very time when she was to be delivered!* His parents were residing at Nazareth; and what should they want to travel at that time for? Naturally, they would have remained home; it was not at all likely that his mother would have taken a journey to Bethlehem while in so peculiar a condition; but Caesar Augustus issues a decree that they are to be taxed. Very well, then, let them be taxed at Nazareth. No; it pleases him that they should all go to their city.

But why should Caesar Augustus think of it just at that particular time? Simply because, while man devises his way, the king's heart is in the hand of the Lord. Why, what a thousand chances, as the world has it, met together to bring about this event! First of all, Caesar quarrels with Herod; one of the Herods was deposed; Caesar says, "I shall tax Judea, and make it a province, instead of having it for a separate kingdom." Well, it must be done. But when is it to be done? This taxing, it is said, was first commenced when Cyreneus was governor. But why is the census to be taken at that particular period—suppose, December? Why not have had it last October? And why could not the people be taxed where they were living? Was not their money just as good there as anywhere else?

It was Caesar's whim; but it was God's decree. Oh! we love the sublime doctrine of eternal absolute predestination. Some have doubted its being consistent with the free agency of man. We know well it is so, and we never saw any difficulty in the subject; we believe metaphysicians have made difficulties; we see none ourselves.

It is for us to believe that man does as he pleases, yet notwithstanding he always does as God decrees. If Judas betrays Christ, "thereunto he was appointed"; and if Pharoah hardens his heart, yet, "for this purpose have I raised thee up, for to show forth my power in thee." Man does as he wills; but God makes him do as *He* wills, too. No, not only is the will of man under the absolute predestination of Jehovah; but all things, great or little, are of Him.

Well has the good poet said, "Doubtless the sailing of a cloud hath Providence to its pilot; doubtless the root of an oak is gnarled for a special purpose, God compasseth all things, mantling the globe like air."

There is nothing great or little that is not from Him. The summer dust moves in its orbit, guided by the same hand which rolls the stars along; the dewdrops have their father, and trickle on the rose leaf as God bids them; yes, the sear leaves of the forest, when hurled along by the tempest, have their allotted position where they shall fall, nor can they go beyond it. In the great, and in the little, there is God—God in everything, working all things according to the counsel of His own will; and though man seeks to go against his Maker, yet he cannot. God has bounded the sea with a barrier of sand; and if the sea mount up wave after wave, yet it shall not exceed its allotted channel. Everything is of God; and to Him who guides the stars and wings sparrows, who rules planets and yet moves atoms, who speaks thunders and yet whispers zephyrs, to Him be glory; for there is God in everything.

What Did Jesus Come For?

For what work did Jesus come? He came to be "ruler in Israel." A very singular thing is this, that Jesus Christ was said to have been born the king of the Jews. Very few have ever been "born king." Men are born princes, but they are seldom born kings. I do not think you can find an instance in history where any infant was born king. He was the prince of Wales, perhaps, and he had to wait a number of years until his father died, and then they manufactured him into a king, by putting a crown on his head; and a sacred chrism, and other silly things; but he was not born a king. I remember no one who was born a king except Jesus; and there is emphatic meaning in that verse that we sing—

> Born thy people to deliver;
> Born a child, and yet a king.

The moment that He came on earth He was a king. He did not wait until His majority that He might take His empire; but as soon as His eye greeted the sunshine He was a king; from the moment that His little hands grasped anything, they grasped a scepter; as soon as His pulse beat, and His blood began to flow, His heart beat royally, and His pulse beat an imperial measure, and His blood flowed in a kingly current. He was born a king. He came "to be ruler in Israel."

"Ah!" says one, "then He came in vain, for little did He exercise His rule; 'he came unto his own, and his own received him not'; He came to Israel and He was not their ruler, but He was 'despised and rejected of men,' cast off by them all, and forsaken by Israel, to whom He came." Ay, but "they are not all Israel who are of Israel," neither because they are the seed of Abraham shall they all be called.

Ah, no! He is not ruler of Israel after the flesh, but He is the ruler of Israel after the spirit. Many such have obeyed Him. Did not the apostles bow before Him, and own Him as their king? And now, does not Israel salute Him as their ruler? Do not all the seed of Abraham after the spirit, even all the faithful, for He is "the father of the faithful," acknowledge that to Christ belong the shields of the mighty, for He is the king of the whole earth? Does He not rule over Israel? Ay, verily He does; and those who are not ruled over by Christ are not of Israel. He came to be a ruler over Israel.

My brother, have you submitted to the sway of Jesus? Is He ruler in your heart, or is He not? We may know Israel by this: Christ is come into their hearts, to be ruler over them. "Oh!" says one, "I do as I please, I was never in bondage to any man" Ah! then you hate the rule of Christ. "Oh!" says another, "I submit myself to my minister, to my clergyman, or to my priest, and I think that what he tells me is enough, for he is my ruler." Do you? Ah! poor slave, you know not your dignity; for nobody is your lawful ruler but the Lord Jesus Christ. "Ay," says another, "I have professed His religion, and I am His follower." But does He rule in your heart? Does He command your will? Does He guide your judgment? Do you ever seek counsel at His hand in your difficulties? Are You desirous to honor him, and to put crowns upon His head? Is He your ruler? If so, then you are one of Israel; for it is written, "He shall come to be ruler in Israel."

Blessed Lord Jesus! You are ruler in Your people's hearts, and You ever shall be; we want no other ruler save Your, and we will submit to none other. We are free, because we are the servants of Christ; we are at liberty, because He is our ruler, and we know no bondage and no slavery, because Jesus Christ alone is monarch of our hearts.

He came to be ruler in Israel; and mark you, that mission of His is not quite fulfilled yet, and shall not be until the latter day glories. In a little while you shall see Christ come again to be ruler over His people Israel, and ruler over them not only as spiritual Israel, but even as natural Israel, for the Jews shall be restored to their land, and the tribes of Jacob shall yet sing in the halls of their temple; to God there shall yet again be offered Hebrew songs of praise, and the heart of the unbelieving Jew shall be melted at the feet of the true Messias. In a short time, He who at His birth was hailed king of the Jews by Easterns, and at His death was written king of the Jews by a Western, shall be called king of the Jews everywhere—yes, king of the Jews and Gentiles also—in that universal monarchy whose dominion shall be coextensive with the habitable globe, and whose duration shall be coeval with time itself. He came to be a ruler in Israel, and a ruler most decidedly He shall be, when He shall reign among His people with His ancients gloriously.

Did Jesus Christ Ever Come Before?

Did Christ come before? We answer, yes: for our text says, "Whose goings forth have been of old, from everlasting."

First, Christ has had His goings forth in His Godhead. "From everlasting." He has not been a secret and a silent person up to this moment. That newborn child there has worked wonders long before now; that infant slumbering in His mother's arms is the infant of today, but it is the ancient of eternity; that child who is there has not made an appearance on the stage of this world; His name is not yet written in the calendar of the circumcised; but still though you wist it not, "his goings forth have been of old, from everlasting."

Of old *He went forth as our covenant head in election*, "according as he hath chosen us in *Him*, before the foundation of the world,"

> Christ be my first elect, he said,
> Then chose our souls in Christ our Head.

He had goings forth for His people, *as their representative before the throne, even before they were begotten in the world*. It was from everlasting that His mighty fingers grasped the pen, the stylus of ages, and wrote His own name, the name of the eternal Son of God; it was from everlasting that He signed the compact with His Father, that He would pay blood for blood, wound for wound, suffering for suffering, agony for agony, and death for death, in the behalf of His people; it was from everlasting that He gave Himself up, without a murmuring word, that from the crown of His head to the sole of His foot He might sweat blood, that He might be spit upon, pierced, mocked, rent asunder, suffer the pain of death, and the agonies of the cross. His goings forth as our Surety were from everlasting.

Pause, my soul, and wonder! You had goings forth in the person of Jesus from everlasting. Not only when you were born into the world did Christ love you, but His delights are with the sons of men before there were any sons of men. Often did He think of them; from everlasting to everlasting He had set His affection upon them. What! believer, has He been so long about your salvation, and will He not accomplish it? Has He from everlasting been going forth to save me, and will He lose me now? What! has He had me in His hand, as His precious jewel, and will He now let me slip between His precious fingers? Did He choose me before the mountains were brought forth, or the channels of the deep scooped out, and will He lose me now? Impossible!

> My name from the palms of his hands
>> Eternity cannot erase;
> Impress'd on his heart it remains,
>> In marks of indelible grace.

I am sure He would not love me so long, and then leave off loving me. If He intended to be tired of me, He would have been tired of me long before now. If He had not loved me with a love as deep as hell and as unutterable as the grave, if He had not given His whole heart to me, I am sure He would have turned from me long ago. He knew what I would be, and He has had long time enough to consider of it; but I am His choice, and there is an end of it; and unworthy as I am, it is not mine to grumble, if He is but contented with me. But He is contented with me—He must be contented with me—for He has known me long enough to know my faults. He knew me before I knew myself; yes, He knew me before I was myself. Long before my members were fashioned they were written in His book, "when as yet there were none of them," His eyes of affection were set on them. He knew how badly I would act toward Him, and yet He has continued to love me;

> His love in times past forbids me to think,
> He'll leave me at last in trouble to sink.

No; since "his goings forth were of old from everlasting," they will be "to everlasting."

Secondly, we believe that Christ *has come forth of old, even to men, so that men have beheld Him.* I will not stop to tell you that it was Jesus who walked in the garden of Eden in the cool of the day, for His delights were with the sons of men; nor will I detain you by pointing out all the various ways in which Christ came forth to His people in the form of the angel of the covenant, the Paschal Lamb, the brazen serpent, the burning bush, and ten thousand types with which the sacred history is so replete; but I will rather point you to four occasions when Jesus Christ our Lord has appeared on earth as a man, before His great incarnation for our salvation.

And, first, I beg to refer you to the eighteenth chapter of Genesis, where Jesus Christ appeared to *Abraham*, of whom we read, "The Lord appeared unto him in the plains of Mamre: and he sat in the tent door in the heat of the day; and he lift up his eyes and looked, and lo, three men stood by him; and when he saw them, he ran to meet them from the tent door, and bowed himself toward the ground!" But whom did he bow to? He said "My lord," only to one of them. There was one man between the other two, the most conspicuous for His glory, for He was the God-man Christ; the other two were created angels, who for a time had assumed the appearance of men. But this was the man Christ Jesus. "And he said, My lord, if now I have found favor in thy sight, pass not away, I pray thee, from thy servant: Let a little water, I pray you, be fetched, and wash your feet, and rest yourselves under the tree." You will notice that this majestic man, this glorious person, stayed behind to talk with Abraham. In the twenty-second verse it is said, "And the men turned their faces from thence and went toward Sodom"; that is, two of them, as you will see in the next chapter, "but Abraham stood yet before the Lord." You will notice that this man, the Lord, held sweet fellowship with Abraham, and allowed Abraham to plead for the city He was about to destroy. He was in the positive form of man; so that when He walked the streets of Judea it was not the first time that He was a man; He was so before, in "the plain of Mamre, in the heat of the day."

There is another instance—His appearing to *Jacob*, which you have recorded in Genesis 32:24. All his family were gone, "And Jacob was left alone, and there wrestled a man with him until the breaking of the day. And when he saw that he prevailed not against him, he touched the hollow of his thigh; and the hollow of Jacob's thigh was out of joint, as he wrestled with him. And he said, Let me go, for the day breaketh. And he said, I will not let thee go, unless thou bless me. And he said unto him, What is thy name? And he said, Jacob. And he said, Thy name shall be called no more Jacob, but Israel; for as a prince hast thou power with God." This was a man, and yet God. "For as a prince hast thou power with God and with men, and hast prevailed." And Jacob knew that this man was God, for he says in the thirtieth verse: "for I have seen God face to face, and my life is preserved."

Another instance you will find in the book of *Joshua*. When Joshua had crossed the narrow stream of Jordan, and had entered the Promised Land, and was about to drive out the Canaanites, lo! this mighty man-God appeared to Joshua. In Joshua 5:13, we read—"And it came to pass, when Joshua was by Jericho, that he lifted up his eyes and looked, and behold, there stood a man over against him with his sword drawn in hi hand, and Joshua went unto him, and [like a brave warrior, as he wa↑ said unto him, Art thou for us, or for our adversaries? And he said, N↑ but as Captain of the host of the Lord am I now come." And Joshua ↑ at once that there was divinity in Him; for Joshua fell on his face tc earth, and did worship, and said to him, "What saith *my lord* unt↑ servant?" Now, if this had been a created angel He would have rep↑ Joshua, and said, "I am one of your fellow servants." But no; "th↑ tain of the Lord's host said unto Joshua, Loose thy shoe from th↑ for the place whereon thou standest is holy. And Joshua did so."

Another remarkable instance is that recorded in the third chapter of the book of Daniel, where we read the account of Shadrach, Meshach, and Abednego being cast into the fiery furnace, which was so fierce that it destroyed the men who threw them in. Suddenly the king said to his counselors—"Did not we cast three men bound into the midst of the fire? They answered and said unto the king, True, O king. He answered and said, Lo, I see four men loose, walking in the midst of the fire, and they have no hurt; and the form of the fourth is like the Son of God." How should Nebuchadnezzar know that? Only that there was some-thing so noble and majestic in the way in which that wondrous Man bore Himself and some awful influence about Him, who so mar-velously broke the consuming teeth of that biting and devouring flame, so that it could not so much as singe the children of God. Nebuchadnezzar recognized his humanity. He did not say, "I see three men and an angel," but he said, "I see four [positive] men, and the form of the fourth is like the Son of God." You see, then, what is meant by His goings forth being "from everlasting."

Observe for a moment here, that each of these four great occurrences happened to the saints *when they were engaged in very eminent duty, or when they were about to be engaged in it.* Jesus Christ does not appear to His saints every day. He did not come to see Jacob until he was in af-fliction; He did not visit Joshua until he was about to be engaged in a righteous war. It is only in extraordinary seasons that Christ thus mani-fests Himself to His people.

When Abraham interceded for Sodom, Jesus was with him, for one of the highest and noblest employments of a Christian is that of inter-cession, and it is when he is so engaged that he will be likely to obtain a sight of Christ. Jacob was engaged in *wrestling*, and that is a part of a Christain's duty to which some of you never did attain; consequently, you do not have many visits from Jesus.

It was when Joshua was *exercising bravery* that the Lord met him. So with Shadrach, Meshach, and Abednego: they were in the high places of *persecution*, on account of their adherence to duty, when He came to them, and said, "I will be with you, passing through the fire." There are certain peculiar places we must enter, to meet with the Lord. We must be in great trouble, like Jacob; we must be in great labor, like Joshua; we must have great intercessory faith, like Abraham; we must be firm in the performance of duty, like Shadrach, Meshach, and Abednego; or else we shall not know Him "whose goings forth have been of old, from everlasting;" or, if we know Him, we shall not be able to "comprehend with all the saints what is the height, and depth, and length, and breadth of the love of Christ, which passeth knowl-edge."

Sweet Lord Jesus! You whose goings forth were of old, even from everlasting, You have not left Your goings forth yet. Oh! that You would go forth this day to cheer the faint, to help the weary, to bind up our wounds, to comfort our distresses! Go forth, we beseech You, to conquer sinners, to subdue hard hearts—to break the iron gates of sinners' lusts, and cut the iron bars of their sins in pieces! O Jesus! go forth; and when You go forth, come to me! Am I a hardened sinner? Come to me; I want You:

> Oh! let thy grace my heart subdue;
> I would be led in triumph too;
> A willing captive to my Lord,
> To sing the honors of thy word.

Poor sinner! Christ has not left going forth yet. And when He goes forth, recollect, He goes to Bethlehem. Have you a Bethlehem in your heart? Are you little, He will go forth to you yet. Go home and seek Him by earnest prayer. If you have been made to weep on account of sin, and think yourself too little to be noticed, go home, little one! Jesus comes to little ones; His goings forth were of old, and He is going forth now. He will come to your poor old house; He will come to your poor wretched heart; He will come, though you are in poverty, and clothed in rags, though you are destitute, tormented, and afflicted; He will come, for His goings forth have been of old from everlasting. Trust Him, trust Him, trust Him; and He will go forth to abide in your heart forever.

4

Holy Work for Christmas

And when they had seen it, they made known abroad the saying which was told them concerning this child. And all they that heard it wondered at those things which were told them by the shepherds. But Mary kept all these things, and pondered them in her heart. And the shepherds returned, glorifying and praising God for all the things that they had heard and seen, as it was told unto them (Luke 2:17–20).

Every season has its own proper fruit: apples for autumn, holly berries for Christmas. The earth brings forth according to the period of the year, and with man there is a time for every purpose under heaven. At this season, the world is engaged in congratulating itself and in expressing its complimentary wishes for the good of its citizens; let me suggest extra and more solid work for Christians. As we think today of the birth of the Savior, let us aspire after a fresh birth of the Savior in our hearts; that as He is already "formed in us the hope of glory," we may be "renewed in the spirit of our minds"; that we may go again to the Bethlehem of our spiritual nativity and do our first works, enjoy our first loves, and feast with Jesus as we did in the holy, happy, heavenly days of our espousals. Let us go to Jesus with something of that youthful freshness and excessive delight which was so manifest in us when we looked to Him at the first; let Him be crowned anew by us, for He is still adorned with the dew of His youth, and remains "the same yesterday, today, and forever."

The citizens of Durham, though they dwell not far from the Scotch border, and consequently in the olden times were frequently liable to be attacked, were exempted from the toils of war because there was a cathedral within their walls, and they were set aside to the bishop's ser-

---

This sermon was taken from *The Metropolitan Tabernacle Pulpit* and was preached on Sunday morning, December 24, 1865.

vice, being called in the olden times by the name of "holy work-folk." Now, we citizens of the New Jerusalem, having the Lord Jesus in our midst, may well excuse ourselves from the ordinary ways of celebrating this season; and considering ourselves to be "holy work-folk," we may keep it after a different sort from other men, in holy contemplation and in blessed service of that gracious God whose unspeakable gift the newborn King is to us.

I selected this text this morning because it seemed to indicate to me four ways of serving God, four methods of executing holy work and exercising Christian thought. Each of the verses sets before us a different way of sacred service. Some, it appears, published abroad the news, told to others what they had seen and heard; some wondered with a holy marveling and astonishment; one, at least, according to the third of the verses, pondered, meditated, thought upon these things; and others, in the fourth place, glorified God and gave Him praise. I know not which of these four did God best service, but I think if we could combine all these mental emotions and outward exercises, we should be sure to praise God after a most godly and acceptable fashion.

Publishing Abroad

To begin then we find that some celebrated the Savior's birth by publishing abroad what they had heard and seen; and truly we may say of them that *they had something* to rehearse in men's ears well worth the telling. That for which prophets and kings had waited long had at last arrived and arrived to them. They had found out the answer to the perpetual riddle. They might have run through the streets with the ancient philosopher, crying, "Eureka! Eureka!" for their discovery was far superior to his. They had found out no solution to a mechanical problem or metaphysical dilemma, but their discovery was second to none ever made by men in real value, since it has been like the leaves of the tree of life to heal the nations, and a river of water of life to make glad the city of God.

They had seen angels; they had heard them sing a song all strange and new. They had seen more than angels—they had beheld the angels' King, the Angel of the Covenant whom we delight in. They had heard the music of heaven, and when near that manger the ear of their faith had heard the music of earth's hope, a mystic harmony which should ring all down the ages—the grave sweet melody of hearts attuned to praise the Lord, and the glorious swell of the holy joy of God and man rejoicing in glad accord. They had seen God incarnate—such a sight that he who gazes on it must feel his tongue unloosed, unless indeed an unspeakable astonishment should make him dumb. Be silent when their eyes had seen such a vision! Impossible! To the first person they met outside that lowly stable door they began to tell their matchless tale, and they wearied not until nightfall, crying, "Come and worship! Come and worship Christ, the newborn King!" As for us, beloved, have we also not something to relate which demands utterance? If we talk of Jesus, who can blame us? This, indeed, might make the tongue of him that sleeps to move—the mystery of God incarnate for our sake, bleeding and dying that we might neither bleed nor die, descending that we might ascend, and wrapped in swaddling bands that we might be unwrapped of the grave-clothes of corruption. Here is such a story, so profitable to all hearers that he who repeats it the most often does best, and he who speaks the least has most reason to accuse himself for sinful silence.

They had something to tell, and *that something had in it the inimitable blending which is the secret sign and royal mark of Divine authorship; a peerless marrying of sublimity and simplicity*; angels singing—singing to shepherds! Heaven bright with glory! bright at midnight! God! A Babe! The Infinite! An Infant of a span long! The Ancient of Days! Born of a woman! What more simple than the inn, the manger, a carpenter, a carpenter's wife, a child? What more sublime than a "multitude of the heavenly host" waking the midnight with their joyous chorales, and God Himself in human flesh made manifest. A child is but an ordinary sight; but what a marvel to see that Word which was "in the beginning with God, tabernacling among us that we might behold his glory—the glory as of the only begotten of the Father, full of grace and truth?" Brethren, we have a tale to tell, as simple as sublime. What simpler?—"Believe and live." What more sublime?—"God was in Christ reconciling the world unto himself!" A system of salvation so wonderful that angelic minds cannot but adore as they meditate upon it; and yet so simple that the children in the temple may fitly hymn its virtues as they sing. "Hosanna! Blessed is he that cometh in the name of the Lord." What a splendid combining of the sublime and the simple have we in the great atonement offered by the incarnate Savior! Oh, make known to all men this saving truth!

The shepherds need no excuse for making everywhere the announcement of the Savior's birth, *for what they told they first received from heaven.* Their news was not muttered in their ears by sibylline oracles, not brought to light by philosophic search, not conceived in poetry, nor found as treasure trove among the volumes of the ancient; but it was revealed to them by that notable Gospel preacher who led the angelic host, and testified, "unto you is born this day, in the city of David, a Savior, which is Christ the Lord." When heaven entrusts a man with a merciful revelation, he is bound to deliver the good tidings to others. What, keep that a secret whose utterance eternal mercy makes to charm the midnight air? To what purpose were angels sent, if the message were not to be spread abroad? According to the teaching of our own beloved Lord we must not be silent, for He bids us, "What ye hear in secret that reveal ye in public; and what I tell you in the ear in closets, that proclaim ye upon the house-tops." Beloved, you have heard a voice from heaven—you twice-born men, begotten again to a lively hope, you have heard the Spirit of God bearing witness of God's truth with you, and teaching you of heavenly things. You then must keep this Christmas by telling to your fellowmen what God's own Holy Spirit has seen fit to reveal to you.

But though the shepherds told what they heard from heaven, remember that *they spoke of what they had seen below.* They had, by observation, made those truths most surely their own which had first been spoken to them by revelation. No man can speak of the things of God with any success until the doctrine which he finds in the Book he finds also in his heart. We must bring down the mystery and make it plain, by knowing, by the teaching of the Holy Spirit, its practical power on the heart and conscience.

My brethren, the Gospel which we preach is most surely revealed to us by the Lord; but, moreover, our hearts have tried and proved, have grasped, have felt, have realized its truth in power. If we have not been able to understand its heights and depths, yet we have felt its mystic power upon our hearts and spirits. It has revealed sin to us better; it has revealed to us our pardon. It has killed the reigning power of sin, it has given us Christ to reign over us, the Holy Spirit to dwell within our bodies as in a temple. Now *we must* speak. I do not urge any of you to speak of Jesus who merely know the Word as you find it in the Bible, your teaching can have but little power; but I do speak earnestly to you who know its mighty influence upon the heart, who have not only heard of the babe but have seen Him in the manger, taken Him up in your own arms and received Him as being born to you, a Savior to you, Christos, the anointed for you, Jesus the Savior from sin for you. Beloved, can you do otherwise than speak of the things which you have seen and heard. God has made you to taste and to handle of this good word of life, and you must not, you dare not hold your peace, but you *must* tell to friends and neighbors what you have felt within.

These were shepherds, *unlettered men.* I will warrant you they could not read in a book; there is no probability that they even knew a single letter. They were shepherds, but they preached right well; and, my brethren, whatever some may think, preaching is not to be confined to those learned gentlemen who have taken their degrees at Oxford or at Cambridge, or at any College or University. It is true that learning need not be an impediment to grace, and may be a fitting weapon in a gracious hand, but often the grace of God has glorified itself by the plain clear way in which unlettered men have understood the Gospel and have proclaimed it. I would not mind asking the whole world to find a Master of Arts now living who has brought more souls to Christ Jesus than Richard Weaver. If the whole bench of bishops have done a tenth as much in the way of soulwinning as that one man, it is more than most of us give them credit for. Let us give to our God all the glory, but still let us not deny the fact that this sinner saved, with the brogue of the collier still about him, fresh from the coal pit, tells the story of the Cross by God's grace in such a way that Right Reverend Fathers in God might humbly sit at his feet to learn the way to reach the heart and melt the stubborn soul. It is true an uneducated brother is not fitted for all work—he has his own sphere—but he is quite able to tell of what he has seen and heard, and so it strikes me is every man in a measure.

If you have seen Jesus and heard His saving voice, if you have re-ceived truth as from the Lord, felt its tremendous power as coming from God to you, and if you have experienced its might upon your own spirit, why you can surely tell out what God has written within. If you cannot get beyond that into the deeper mysteries, into the more knotty points, well, well, there are some who can, and so you need not be un-easy; but you can at least reveal the first and foundation truths, and they are by far the most important. If you cannot speak in the pulpit, if as yet your cheek would mantle with a blush, and your tongue would refuse to do her office in the presence of many, there are your children, you are not ashamed to speak before them; there is the little cluster around the hearth on Christmas night, there is the little congregation in the work-shop, there is a little audience somewhere to whom you might tell out of Jesus' love to lost ones.

Do not get beyond what you know; do not plunge into what you have not experienced, for if you do you will be out of your depth, and then very soon you will be floundering and making confusion worse con-founded. Go as far as you know; and since you do know yourself a sinner and Jesus a Savior, and a great one too, talk about those two matters, and good will come of it. Beloved, each one in his own position, tell what you have heard and seen; publish that abroad among the sons of men.

But *were they authorized?* It is a great thing to be authorized! Unauthorized ministers are most shameful intruders! Unordained men entering the pulpit who are not in the apostolical succession—very hor-rible! Very horrible indeed! The Puseyite mind utterly fails to fathom the depth of horror which is contained in the idea of an unauthorized man preaching, and a man out of the apostolical succession daring to teach the way of salvation. To me this horror seems very like a school-boy's fright at a hobgoblin which his fears had conjured up. I think if I saw a man slip through the ice into a cold grave, and I could rescue him from drowning, it would not be so very horrible to me to be the means of saving him, though I may not be employed by the Royal Humane Society. I imagine if I saw a fire and heard a poor woman scream at an upper window and likely to be burned alive, if I should wheel the fire escape up to the window, and preserve her life, it would not be so very dreadful a matter though I might not belong to the regular Fire Brigade. If a company of brave volunteers should chase an enemy out of their own county, I do not know that it would be anything so shocking, although a whole army of mercenaries might be neglecting their work in obedience to some venerable military rubric which rendered them incapable of effective service.

But mark you, the shepherds and others like them are in the apostolical succession, and they are authorized by divine ordinance, for every man who hears the Gospel is authorized to tell it to others. Do you want authority? Here it is in confirmation strong from Holy Writ: "Let him that heareth say, Come"—that is, let every man who truly hears the Gospel bid others come to drink of the water of life. This is all the warrant you require for preaching the Gospel according to your ability. It is not every man who has ability to preach the Word; and it is not every man that we should like to hear preach it in the great congregation, for if all were mouth, what a great vacuum the church would be; yet every Christian in some method should deliver the glad tidings. Our wise God takes care that liberty of prophesying shall not run to riot, for He does not give efficient pastoral and ministerial gifts to very many; yet every man according to his gifts, let him minister. Every one of you though not in the pulpit, yet in the pew, in the workshop, somewhere, anywhere, everywhere, do make known the savor of the Lord Jesus. Be this your authority: "Let him that heareth say, Come." I never thought of asking any authority for crying "Fire!" when I saw a house burning; I never dreamed of seeking any authority for doing my best to rescue a poor perishing fellowman, nor do I mean to seek it now! All the authority you want, any of you, is not the authority which can stream from prelates decorated with lawn sleeves, but the authority which comes direct from the great Head of the church, who gives authority to every one of those who hear the Gospel, to teach every man his fellow; saying, "Know the Lord."

Here, dear brethren, is one way for you to keep a right holy, and in some sense a right merry, Christmas. Imitate these humble men of whom it is said, "When they had seen it they made known abroad the saying which was told them concerning the child."

Holy Wonder, Admiration, and Adoration

We set before you, now, another mode of keeping Christmas, by holy wonder, admiration, and adoration. "And all they that heard it wondered at those things which were told them by the shepherds." We shall have little to say of those persons who merely wondered and did nothing more. Many are set a wondering by the Gospel. They are content to hear it, pleased to hear it; if not in itself something new, yet there are new ways of putting it, and they are glad to be refreshed with the variety. The preacher's voice is to them as the sound of one that gives a goodly tune upon an instrument. They are glad to listen. They are not skeptics, they do not cavil, they raise no difficulties; they just say to themselves, "It is an excellent Gospel, it is a wonderful plan of salvation. Here is most astonishing love, most extraordinary condescension." Sometimes they marvel that these things should be told them by shepherds; they can hardly understand how unlearned and ignorant men should speak of these things, and how such things should ever get into these shepherds' heads, where they can have learned them, how it is that they seem so earnest about them, what kind of operation they must have passed through to be able to speak as they do. But after holding up their hands and opening their mouths for about nine days, the wonder subsides, and they go their way and think no more about it.

There are many of you who are set a wondering whenever you see a work of God in your district. You hear of somebody converted who was a very extraordinary sinner, and you say, "It is very wonderful!" There is a revival; you happen to be present at one of the meetings when the Spirit of God is working gloriously. You say, "Well, this is a singular thing! very astonishing!" Even the newspapers can afford a corner at times for very great and extraordinary works of God the Holy Spirit; but there all emotion ends; it is all wondering, and nothing more.

Now, I trust it will not be so with any of us; that we shall not think of the Savior and of the doctrines of the Gospel which He came to preach simply with amazement and astonishment, for this will work us but little good. On the other hand, there is another mode of wondering which is akin to adoration, if it be not adoration. I think it would be very difficult to draw a line between holy wonder and real worship, for when the soul is overwhelmed with the majesty of God's glory, though it may not express itself in song, or even utter its voice with bowed head in humble prayer, yet it silently adores. I am inclined to think that the astonishment which sometimes seizes upon the human intellect at the remembrance of God's greatness and goodness is, perhaps, the purest form of adoration which ever rises from mortal men to the throne of the Most High. This kind of wonder I recommend to those of you who from the quietness and solitariness of your lives are scarcely able to imitate the shepherds in telling out the tale to others. You can at least fill up the circle of the worshipers before the throne by wondering at what God has done.

Let me suggest to you that holy wonder at what God has done should be very natural to you. That God should consider His fallen creature, man, and instead of sweeping him away with the besom of destruction should devise a wonderful scheme for his redemption, and that He should Himself undertake to be man's Redeemer, and to pay his ransom price, is, indeed, marvelous!

Probably it is most marvelous to you in its relation to yourself; that you should be redeemed by blood; that God should forsake the thrones and royalties above to suffer ignominiously below for you. If you know yourself you can never see any adequate motive or reason in your own flesh for such a deed as this. "Why such love to me?" you will say. If David sitting in his house could only say, "Who am I, O Lord God, and what is mine house, that thou hast brought me hitherto?"

What should you and I say? Had we been the most meritorious of individuals, and had unceasingly kept the Lord's commands, we could not have deserved such a priceless boon as incarnation; but sinners, offenders, who revolted and went from God, further and further, what shall we say of this incarnate God dying for us, but "Herein is love, not that we loved God but that he loved us."

Let your soul lose itself in wonder, for wonder, dear friends, is in this way a very practical emotion. Holy wonder will lead you to grateful worship; being astonished at what God has done, you will pour out your soul with astonishment at the foot of the golden throne with the song, "Blessing, and honor, and glory, and majesty, and power, and dominion, and might be unto him who sitteth on the throne and doeth these great things to me."

Filled with this wonder it will cause you a godly watchfulness; you will be afraid to sin against such love as this. Feeling the presence of the mighty God in the gift of His dear Son, you will put off your shoes from off your feet, because the place whereon you stand is holy ground. You will be moved at the same time to a glorious hope. If Jesus has given Himself to you, if He has done this marvelous thing on your behalf, you will feel that heaven itself is not too great for your expectation, and that the rivers of pleasure at God's right hand are not too sweet or too deep for you to drink thereof.

Who can be astonished at anything when he has once been astonished at the manger and the Cross? What is there wonderful left after one has seen the Savior? The nine wonders of the world! Why, you may put them all into a nutshell—machinery and modern art can excel them all; but this one wonder is not the wonder of earth only, but of heaven and earth, and even hell itself. It is not the wonder of the olden time, but the wonder of all time and the wonder of eternity. They who see human wonders a few times at last cease to be astonished; the noblest pile that architect ever raised at last fails to impress the onlooker; but not so this marvelous temple of incarnate Deity; the more we look the more we are astonished, the more we become accustomed to it, the more have we a sense of its surpassing splendor of love and grace. There is more of God, let us say, to be seen in the manger and the Cross than in the sparkling stars above, the rolling deep below, the towering mountain, the teeming valleys, the abodes of life, or the abyss of death. Let us then spend some choice hours of this festive season in holy wonder, such as will produce gratitude, worship, love, and confidence.

Her Sacred Heart Pondering and Preserving

One at least, and let us hope there were others, or at any rate let us ourselves be others—one kept all these things and pondered them in her heart. She wondered: she did more—she pondered. You will observe there was an exercise on the part of this blessed woman of the three great parts of her being; her memory—she kept all these things; her affections—she kept them in her heart; her intellect—she pondered them, considered them, weighed them, turned them over; so that memory, affection, and understanding were all exercised about these things. We delight to see this in Mary, but we are not at all surprised when we recollect that she was in some sense the most concerned of all on earth, for it was of her that Jesus Christ had been born.

Those who come nearest to Jesus and enter the most closely into fellowship with Him will be sure to be the most engrossed with Him. Certain persons are best esteemed at a distance, but not the Savior; when you shall have known Him to the very full, then shall you love Him with the love which passes knowledge; you shall comprehend the heights, and depths, and lengths, and breadths of His love; and when you shall do so, then your own love shall swell beyond all length and breadth, all height and depth.

The birth most concerned Mary, and therefore she was the most impressed with it. Note the way in which her concern was shown; she was a woman, and the grace which shines best in the female is not boldness—that belongs to the masculine mind; but affectionate modesty is a feminine beauty, and hence we do not read so much of her telling abroad as pondering within. No doubt she had her circle, and her word to speak in it; but for the most part she, like another Mary, sat still in the house. She worked, but her work was most directly for *Him*, her heart's joy and delight. Like other children, the holy child needed care, which only a mother's hand and heart could exercise; she was therefore engrossed with Him.

O blessed engrossment! Sweet engagement! Count not that to be unacceptable service which occupies itself rather with Jesus than with His disciples or His wandering sheep. That woman who broke the alabaster box and poured the ointment upon our Jesus Himself was blamed by Judas, and even the rest of the disciples thought that the poor had lost a benefit, but "she hath wrought a good work on me" was the Savior's answer. I desire to bring you to this thought, that if during this season you retiring quiet ones cannot speak to others, or have no desirable opportunity or suitable gift for that work, you may sit still with Jesus and honor Him in peace. Mary took the Lord in her arms; oh, that you may bear Him in yours! She executed works for His person directly; do you imitate her. You can love Him, bless Him, praise Him, study Him, ponder Him, comprehend His character, study the types that set Him forth, and imitate His life; and in this way, though your worship will not blaze forth among the sons of men, and scarcely benefit them as some other forms of work, yet it will both benefit you and be acceptable to your Lord.

Beloved, remember what you have heard of Christ, and what He has done for you; make your heart the golden cup to hold the rich recollections of His past loving-kindness; make it a pot of manna to preserve the heavenly bread whereon saints have fed in days gone by. Let your memory treasure up everything about Christ which you have either heard, or felt, or known, and then let your fond affections hold Him fast evermore. Love Him! Pour out that alabaster box of your heart, and let all the precious ointment of your affection come streaming on His feet.

If you cannot do it with joy do it sorrowfully, wash His feet with tears, wipe them with the hairs of your head; but do love Him, love the blessed Son of God, your ever tender Friend. Let your intellect be exercised concerning the Lord Jesus. Turn over and over by meditation what you read. Do not be lettermen—do not stop at the surface; dive into the depths. Be not as the swallow which touches the brook with her wing, but as the fish which penetrates the lowest wave. Drink deep draughts of love; do not sip and away, but dwell at the well as Isaac did at the well Lahai-roi. Abide with your Lord; let Him not be to you as a wayfaring man that tarries for a night, but constrain Him, saying, "Abide with us, for the day is far spent." Hold Him, and do not let Him go.

The word *ponder,* as you know, means "to weigh." Make ready the scales of judgment. Oh, but where are the scales that can weigh the Lord Christ? "He taketh up the isles as a very little thing"—who shall take Him up? "He weigheth the mountains in scales." In what scales shall we weigh *Him*? Be it so, if your understanding cannot comprehend, let your affections apprehend; and if your spirit cannot compass the Lord Jesus in the arms of its understanding, let it embrace Him in the arms of your affection. Oh, beloved, here is blessed Christmas work for you, if like Mary, you lay up all these things in your heart and ponder upon them.

Glorifying and Praising God

The last piece of holy Christmas work is to come. "The shepherds returned," we read in the twentieth verse, "glorifying and praising God for all the things that they had heard and seen, as it was told unto them." Returned to what? Returned to business to look after the lambs and sheep again. Then if we desire to glorify God we need not give up our business.

Some people get the notion into their heads that the only way in which they can live for God is by becoming ministers, missionaries, or Bible women. Alas! how many of us would be shut out from any opportunity of magnifying the Most High if this were the case. The shepherds went back to the sheep pens glorifying and praising God. Beloved, it is not office, it is earnestness; it is not position, it is grace which will enable us to glorify God. God is most surely glorified in that cobbler's stall where the godly worker as he plies the awl sings of the Savior's love, aye, glorified far more than in many a prebendal stall where official *religiousness* performs its scanty duties. The name of Jesus is glorified by yonder carter as he drives his horse and blesses his God, or speaks to his fellow laborer by the roadside, as much as by yonder divine who, throughout the country like Boanerges, is thundering out the Gospel.

God is glorified by our abiding in our vocations. Take care you do not fall out of the path of duty by leaving your calling, and take care you do not dishonor your profession while in it; think not much of yourselves, but do not think too little of your callings. There is no trade which is not sanctified by the Gospel. If you turn to the Bible, you will find the most menial forms of labor have been in some way or other connected either with the most daring deeds of faith, or else with persons whose lives have been otherwise illustrious; keep to your calling, brother, keep to your calling! Whatever God has made you, when He calls you abide in that, unless you are quite sure, mind that, unless you are quite sure that He calls you to something else. The shepherds glorified God though they went to their trade.

They glorified God *though they were shepherds*. As we remarked, they were not men of learning. So far from having an extensive library full of books, it is probable they could not read a word; yet they glorified God. This takes away all excuse for you good people who say, I am no scholar; I never had any education, I never even went to Sunday school." Ah, but if your heart is right, you can glorify God. Never mind, Sarah, do not be cast down because you know so little; learn more if you can, but make good use of what you do know. Never mind, John; it is indeed a pity that you should have had to toil so early, as not to have acquired even the rudiments of knowledge; but do not think that you cannot glorify God. If you would praise God, live a holy life; you can do that by His grace, at any rate, without scholarship. If you would do good to others, be good yourself; and that is a way which is as open to the most illiterate as it is to the best taught. Be of good courage! Shepherds glorified God, and so may you. Remember there is one thing in which they had a preference over the wise men. The wise men wanted a star to lead them; the shepherds did not. The wise men went wrong even with a star, stumbled into Jerusalem; the shepherds went straight away to Bethlehem. Simple minds sometimes find a glorified Christ where learned heads, much puzzled with their lore, miss Him. A good doctor used to say, "Lo, these simpletons have entered into the kingdom, while we learned men have been fumbling for the latch." It is often so; and so, ye simple minds, be ye comforted and glad.

The way in which these shepherds honored God is worth noticing. They did it by praising Him. Let us think more of sacred song than we sometimes do. When the song is bursting in full chorus from the thousands in this house, it is but a noise in the ear of some men; but inasmuch as many true hearts, touched with the love of Jesus, are keeping pace with their tongues, it is not a mere noise in God's esteem, there is a sweet music in it that makes glad His ear. What is the great ultimatum of all Christian effort? When I stood here the other morning preaching the Gospel, my mind was fully exercised with the winning of souls, but I seemed while preaching to get beyond that. I thought, Well, that is not the chief end after all—the chief end is to glorify God, and even the saving of sinners is sought by the right-minded as the means to that end.

Then it struck me all of a sudden, "If in psalm singing and hymn singing we do really glorify God, we are doing more than in the preaching; because we are not then in the means, we are close upon the great end itself." If we praise God with heart and tongue we glorify Him in the surest possible manner, we are really glorifying Him then. "Whoso offereth praise glorifieth me," says the Lord. Sing then, my brethren! Sing not only when you are together but sing alone. Cheer your labor with psalms, and hymns, and spiritual songs. Make glad the family with sacred music. We sing too little, I am sure, yet the revival of religion has always been attended with the revival of Christian psalmody. Luther's translations of the psalms were of as much service as Luther's discussions and controversies; and the hymns of Charles Wesley, and Cennick, and Toplady, and Newton, and Cowper, aided as much in the quickening of spiritual life in England as the preaching of John Wesley and George Whitefield. We want more singing. Sing more and murmur less, sing more and slander less, sing more and cavil less, sing more and mourn less. God grant us today, as these shepherds did, to glorify God by praising Him.

I have not quite done with them. What was the subject of their praise? It appears that they *praised God for what they had heard.* If we think of it, there is good reason for blessing God every time we hear a Gospel sermon. What would souls in hell give if they could hear the Gospel once more, and be on terms in which salvation grace might come to them? What would dying men give whose time is all but over if they could once more come to the house of God, and have another warning and another invitation? My brethren, what would you give sometimes when you are shut up by sickness and cannot meet with the great congregation, when your heart and your flesh cry out for the living God? Well, praise God for what you have heard. You have heard the faults of the preacher; let him mourn them. You have heard his Master's message, do you bless God for that? Scarcely will you ever hear a sermon which may not make you sing if you are in a right mind.

George Herbert says, "Praying is the end of preaching" So it is, but praising is its end too. Praise God that you hear there is a Savior! Praise God that you hear that the plan of salvation is very simple! Praise God that you have a Savior for your own soul! Praise God that you are pardoned, that you are saved!

Praise Him for what you have heard, but observe, *they also praised God for what they had seen.* Look at the twentieth verse—"heard and seen." There is the sweetest music—what we have experienced, what we have felt within, what we have made our own—the things that we have made touching the King. Mere hearing may make some music, but the soul of song must come from seeing with the eye of faith. And, dear friends, you who have seen with that God-given eyesight, I pray you, let not your tongues be steeped in sinful silence, but loud to the praise of sovereign grace, wake up your glory and awake psaltery and harp.

One point for which they praised God was *the agreement between what they had heard and what they had seen.* Observe the last sentence. "As it was told them." Have you not found the Gospel to be in yourselves just what the Bible said it would be? Jesus said He would give you grace—have you not had it? He promised you rest—have you not received it? He said that you should have joy, and comfort, and life through believing in Him—have you not had all these? Are not His ways ways of pleasantness, and His paths paths of peace? Surely you can say with the queen of Sheba, "The half has not been told me."

I have found Christ more sweet than His servants could set Him forth as being. I looked upon the likeness as they painted it, but it was a mere daub as compared with Himself—the King in His beauty. I have heard of the goodly land, but oh! it flows with milk and honey more richly and sweetly than men were ever able to tell me when in their best trim for speech. Surely, what we have seen keeps pace with what we have heard.

Let us then glorify and praise God for what He has done.

This word to those who are not yet converted, and I have done. I do not think you can begin at the seventeenth verse, but I wish you would begin at the eighteenth. You cannot begin at the seventeenth—you cannot tell to others what you have not felt; do not try it. Neither teach in the Sunday school, nor attempt to preach if you are not converted. To the wicked God says, "What hast thou to do to declare my statutes?" But I would to God you would begin with the eighteenth verse—wondering! Wondering that you are spared—wondering that you are out of hell—wondering that His good Spirit still does strive with the chief of sinners. Wonder that this morning the Gospel should have a word for you after all your rejections of it and sins against God. I should like you to begin there because then I would have good hope that you would go on to the next verse and change the first letter, and so go from wondering to pondering. Oh, sinner, I wish you would ponder the doctrines of the Cross. Think of your sin, God's wrath, judgment, hell, your Savior's blood, God's love, forgiveness, acceptance, heaven—think on these things. Go from wondering to pondering. And then I would to God you could go on to the next verse, from pondering to glorifying. Take Christ, look to Him, trust Him. Then sing "I am forgiven," and go your way a believing sinner, and therefore a sinner saved, washed in the blood, and clean. Then go back after that to the seventeenth verse, and begin to tell to others.

But as for you who are saved, I want you to begin this very afternoon at the seventeenth.

> Then will I tell to sinners round
> What a dear Savior I have found:
> I'll point to thy redeeming blood,
> And say—"Behold the way to God!"

Then when the day is over get up to your chambers and wonder, admire and adore; spend half an hour also like Mary in pondering and treasuring up the day's work and the day's hearing in your hearts, and then close all with that which never must close—go on tonight, tomorrow, and all the days of your life, glorifying and praising God for all the things that you have seen and heard. May the Master bless you for Jesus Christ's sake. Amen.

5

The Best Christmas Fare

How sweet are thy words unto my taste! yes, sweeter than honey to my mouth! (Psalm 119:103).

This is a time of feasting, and we may as well have our feast as other people have theirs. Let us see whether there is not something for our spiritual palate, something to satisfy our spiritual appetite, that we may eat, and be content, and rejoice before the Lord. Do you not think that two of the words in our text are very strange? If you had written them, would you not have said, "How sweet are thy words unto my *ear*"? The psalmist says, "How sweet are thy words unto my *palate!*" for that is the word in the margin. He did not write, "Yea, sweeter than honey to my *hearing!*" but, "sweeter than honey to my *mouth!*" Are words, then, things that we can taste and eat? No, not if they are the words of man; it would take many of our words to fill a hungry belly. "Be ye warmed and filled": it would take many tons of that sort of fodder to feed "a brother or sister destitute of daily food," for man's words are air and airy, light and frothy. They often deceive, they mock, they awaken hopes which are never realized; but God's words are full of substance, they are spirit, they are life, they are to be fed upon by the spiritually hungry.

Marvel not that I say this to you. It was God's word that made us; is it any wonder that His word should sustain us? If His word gives life, do you wonder that His word should also give food for that life? Marvel not, for it is written: "Man shall not live by bread alone, but by every word that proceedeth out of the mouth of God." God's words are meat, and drink, and food; and if bodies live not upon words, souls and spirits feed upon the words of God, and so are satisfied, and full of delight. This is the language of an eater as well as of a hearer, of one who

---

This sermon was taken from *The Metropolitan Tabernacle Pulpit* and was preached on the evening of Christmas Day, 1881.

heard the words, and then ate the words. The expression is oriental, but we are not quite strangers to it, even in our western talk, for we say, "They seem to eat the man's words"; that is, when the hearers are very attentive to them, when they enjoy them, when the preacher's words seem to comfort them, and to minister sustenance to their mind and to their spirit.

I like this way of describing the reception of God's word as a matter of eating, for a man cannot eat God's word without living. He that takes it into himself must live thereby. There is a reality about the faith which eats; there is a something there most sure, which contains the elements of salvation, for tasting is a spiritual sense which implies nearness. You can hear at a great distance by means of the telephone; but, somehow, I do not think that anyone will invent an electrical taster. Nobody knows what may be done; but I fancy that I shall never be able to eat anything in New York. I think that we shall hardly ever reach such a triumph of science as that. There will always have to be a measure of nearness if we are to taste anything, and so it is with God's word. If we hear it, it is music in the ear; but still it may seem to be at a distance from us. We may not get a grip and grasp of it; but if we taste it, that means that we really have it here within ourselves. Then has it come very near to us, and we enter into fellowship with the God who gave it.

This idea of tasting God's word contains the thought of receptiveness. A man may hear a thing and, as we say, it goes in at one ear and out at the other, and so it does often; but that which a man gets into his mouth until he tastes it, and it is sweet to his palate, well, he has received that. If it be sweet to him, he will not do as they who have something lukewarm, which is objectionable, which they cast away out of their mouths; but when he finds it palatable, the sweetness will make him keep it where it is until he swallows it down into his inward parts. So I love this thought of tasting God's word, because it implies nearness, and it implies an actual reception, and a veritable holding fast of that which is so appreciated by the taste.

Tasting is also a personal matter. "Friends, Romans, countrymen," said Mark Antony, in his oration over the body of Caesar, "lend me your ears"; and they go to be lent, and numbers of people hear for others. But tasting, surely, is a personal business; there is no possibility of my eating for you. If you choose to starve yourself by a long fast of fifty days, so you must. If I were to sit down, and industriously attempt to eat your portion of food, and my own, too, it would not avail you in the least; you must eat for yourselves, and there is no knowing the value of God's word until you eat it for yourself. You must personally believe it, personally trust to it, personally receive it into your innermost spirit, or else you cannot know anything about its power to bless and to sustain. I do pray, dear friends, that we may every one of us, tonight, understand what the psalmist meant when he spoke of tasting God's words, and of finding them sweeter than honey to his mouth.

An Exclamation

First, tonight, I call your attention to an exclamation. The text contains two notes of exclamation or admiration: "How sweet are thy words unto my taste! yes, sweeter than honey to my mouth!" I cannot throw the notes of admiration and exclamation into my speech as I would like to do; but this verse is evidently the utterance of one who is somewhat surprised and amazed, one who has a thought which he cannot adequately express. The thought is also one that gives much delight to the writer, for he exclaims, "How sweet are thy words unto my taste! yes, sweeter than honey to my mouth!"

Now, I believe that it is a matter of wonder to many to find *the Gospel so sweet when the soul first tastes it.* Until I believed in Christ, I could not have imagined that a man was capable of so much delight as I then experienced. When I first looked to Christ, and was lightened, the ease I felt when my burden rolled from off my shoulder quite astonished me. It seemed to me as if a man could never know such rest as I then enjoyed. When I beheld my sin all put away through Christ's atoning blood, and knew myself to be "accepted in the Beloved," I could have said, with the queen of Sheba, "Behold, the half was not told me." I had heard my father and other Christian men say that blessed are the people who trust in the Lord, but I never thought there really was such blessedness as I found. I fancied that they would decoy me with some sweet declarations of what, after all, might be very commonplace, but I did not find it to be so; and I am here to bear my witness that, when I believed God's promise, I was so amazed and overpowered with joy that, even now, I cannot tell you the delight I felt, aye, and still do feel, in the word of a faithful God to all who trust in Jesus Christ, His Son.

This, then, may be the exclamation of a soul tasting the Gospel for the first time; but it may also be the exclamation of *a soul cheered by still tasting the Gospel*: "How sweet are thy words unto my taste!" "I have known the Lord," says one, "these forty years." Another says, "I have known Christ these thirty years; but He is as precious to me as ever He was, His word is as fresh and novel as if I had never heard it before, and His promise comes to my soul with as much of life and power as if He had only spoken it yesterday, and I had never heard it until this moment." Are you not surprised, sometimes, you who are getting into middle life, or even verging on old age, to find how sweet God's word still is to you? And if, perhaps, you have been away from the house of God traveling in foreign lands, or you have been laid aside by sickness, or, if, perchance, you are a preacher, and do not often hear a sermon, is it not a very delightful thing to sit in your pew, and when you are hearing the Gospel, to say, "Oh, it is sweet! It is coming home to me now"? I heard a sermon, some years ago—I do not often get the opportunity of hearing—and, when my tears began to flow under a simple statement of the Gospel, I said to myself, "Yes, I am not a mere dealer in it, who hands it out to others, for I relish the flavor of it myself." Why, I have had to stand here, sometimes, like the butchers at Christmas time, cutting and chopping off joints of meat for you all, and I have not had even a snack myself all the while; but when I get the opportunity of sitting down at the table, and listening, it may be, to a poor, humble preacher talking about Christ, I seem to set my knife and fork to work, and I say, "Yes, that is just the very food for me, give me some more of it. My soul can feed upon such fare as that"; and I have felt glad, with an inward and unspeakable delight, to find how sweet it was to my taste; "yes, sweeter than honey to my mouth!" Rejoice, dear friends, if you find it so.

I reckon that this language of exclamation and admiration will also come from *the most advanced saint, increasing in knowledge of the Gospel,* the believer who has studied the Word of God most earnestly, and who has had the deepest experience in it. Other books are soon done with, but the Bible is never fully understood. I think that most readers will tell you that the more they read the fewer books become; whereas, to the young, there is a whole library yet to go through. The man who has been a diligent and careful reader all his life finds only some few books that he now cares to read. He knows the rest, he could write the most of them; perhaps, could write them better than they are written. Now he keeps on striking out this one from the list, and that other, for he has gone beyond them; and the book which charmed him when he was young ceases to have any value to him when he gets beyond it in his riper years. He has seen through its mistakes, and now he yearns for something more accurate; but it is never so with the words of God.

It is never so with *the* Word of God, the Incarnate Word, the Christ. The more you know of Him, the more you wish to know; and the more you taste of Him, the sweeter He becomes until, in heaven, the sweetness will be far more intense than it is now, and Christ will be more precious and more delightful to us through the eternal ages than He is at this present moment. I believe that in glory the saints will often lift up their hands, and say, "How sweet are thy words to my taste! yes, sweeter than honey to my mouth!" When those words shall have been completely fulfilled, the very retrospect of the promise will charm our immortal spirits, until heaven shall become as a wood, like that of Jonathan, which dripped with honey; and every word that God spoke to us when we were here below shall come back to us with matchless sweetness as we remember it in the world to come.

A Statement

But now, secondly, take the text not only with its two notes of admiration, but as a statement, a cool statement of matters of fact. David is one who, when his heart boils with holy fervor and his hand wields the pen of a ready writer, still writes accurately. He never speaks more than the truth even when he is most emphatic, so that I am sure that David means to tell us here that God's words were sweet to him.

First, *they were unutterably sweet*: "How sweet!" but he does not tell us how sweet they were. He says, "How sweet are thy words unto my taste!" as if he could not tell us what delightfulness he found in the teachings of God's word; it was unutterable. We can tell you, dear hearers, that God's words of promise are very, very sweet; but we can convey to you no sort of idea of how great that sweetness is. Oh, taste for yourselves, and see that the Lord is good! There is no describing the flavors of a royal banquet, there is no picturing to a man who has not the sense of smell the fragrance of a delicious perfume; and you must personally know the sweetness of the word of God, for to us it is positively unutterable.

This much, however, the psalmist does utter. He tells us that God's words are *surpassingly sweet*, for, says he, "They are sweeter than honey." Honey is supposed to be the sweetest of all known substances. So David means that if there is anything that can delight the heart of man, God's word could charm his heart better than that. David means that if there is anything that could cheer a man, God's word could comfort him better than any other consolation. If there be joy, if there be peace, if there be rest, if there be bliss, to be found in anything else, all that, and more than that, can be found in a higher degree in the teachings of God's word, and in the blessing of the covenant of grace. Sweeter than sweetness itself, sweeter than the sweetest thing that God Himself has made, is God's word which He has spoken. Oh, that we did but know how to taste it!

The psalmist also makes this statement, that *all God's word's are thus unutterably sweet to him*. He does not say that they are so to all men; but He says, "How sweet are thy words unto my taste! yea, sweeter than honey to my mouth!" He speaks thus of all God's words. We know some people who love God's promises, but they do not cure much about His precepts. If God speaks a word of grace, they like that; but if it is a word of command, they do not care about that. Oh, brothers and sisters, I hope we have a taste for every word that God has spoken! A man ought not to say, "I do not like a sermon from the Old Testament so much as I do a sermon from the New Testament." There must be no picking and choosing with God's word. It is virtually atheism when men begin to set one word of God over against another, for the man who dares to criticize God's revelation makes himself greater than God, and therein he has undeified the Deity, and there is no God to him. My God is such to me that, if I know a word to be inspired by His Spirit, I value it beyond all conception. It is not for me to say, "This word of my Master is nothing compared with another word." All those words came from the same mouth; and, coming from the same mouth, they are all equally true to me; and, if not all alike rich in comfort, yet "all Scripture is given by inspiration of God, and is profitable for doctrine, for reproof, for correction, for instruction in righteousness." From one end of it to the other, it answers some divine purpose; and who am I that I should sit in judgment upon it? I pray you, brothers and sisters, value every word of God, and let no man lead you into the error of setting this one above the other; for, if they be God's words, they are all precious, and you ought to count them so.

David seems to say that *God's words are precious to him at all times.* They were sweet to him when he wrote the text; and I cannot tell in what condition of body and mind he was at that time; but this I do know, lying upon the bed of sickness, racked with pain, many of God's saints have said, "How sweet are thy words unto my taste!" And this also I do know, that, lifted up with gratitude for the blessings of providence—health, wealth, friends, yet God's saints have found greater sweetness in His word than in all temporal things; and they have still said, "How sweet are thy words unto my taste!" This is an abiding mark of a child of God, that God's words are sweet to him, aye, sometimes very sweet even when he is half afraid to partake of them! "Oh," says he "would God they were mine! I want nothing sweeter than God's word; and, even if I am a little fearful of appropriating it to myself, yet still it is very, very dear to me." If the name of Jesus is sweeter than honey to your taste, then be glad for this is a mark of a child of God that never failed yet, and never will fail while the world stands.

A Repetition

Now, thirdly, look at the text again, and you will see that it contains a repetition: "How sweet are thy words unto my taste!" Well, that is all right, David; we understand you. "Yes, sweeter than honey to my mouth!" Why do you want to say that? Is not that saying the same thing twice over? Yes, and intentionally so, because God's word is sweet to His people in many ways, and many times over.

As I have already said to you, it is very sweet in its *reception.* When we first take it into our hearts and feed upon it, it is very precious; but, spiritually, men are something like ruminating animals, they have the power of feeding again, and again, and again on that which they have once received. See how the cattle lie down, and chew the cud; and it is when they chew the cud, I suppose, that they get the sweetness out of that which they have eaten. And so, spiritually, when men have once received Christ, they get increasing sweetness out of Him by *meditation*. Having taken Him into their souls, they afterward inwardly digest the precious word, and get the secret juice and latent sweetnesses out of the promises of God's most holy revelation and out of Jesus Christ Himself. It is thus that the psalmist first says, "How sweet are thy words unto my taste!" And then he rolls them around again in his mouth by meditation, and so he repeats himself as he says, "Yes, sweeter than honey to my mouth!"

But do you not think that the repetition in the text means something else, namely, that while, first of all, Christ's word is very sweet to our taste, there is another sweetness when we get it into our mouths, not so much for our own eating, as speaking of it to others? There is great sweetness about the *declaration* of God's words. Some of you who love the Lord have never yet told anybody. You are secret Christians, you hide away behind pillar and post. Oh, but God's word is very sweet to you, you say, as you eat your morsel of bread in the corner! So it is, but you would have another and a greater sweetness if you would come out and avow that you love the Lord. I am sure you would. In fact, there is many a child of God who never does enjoy the full sweetness of religion because he has not had the courage to confess Christ before men. I wish that some of you halting ones, you who are much afraid and fearing, would obey the whole of the Gospel. You know the Gospel is, "He that believeth and is baptized shall be saved." "With the heart man believeth unto righteousness; and with the mouth confession is made unto salvation."

Now, obey the whole of the Gospel; then you shall get the whole of its sweetness. But, perhaps, there is some peculiar flavor in the word which you have never known as yet, because you have been disobedient children. Did you ever notice that saying of our Lord, "Come unto me, all ye that labor and are heavy laden, and I will give you rest"? Yes, you know all about that, you say. Christ says to you, "Come unto me, and I will give you rest." Now go a little farther; what is the next verse? "Take my yoke upon you, and learn of me; and ye shall find rest." Why, that is another rest! I thought you had rest; did not Jesus say that He would give you rest? Yet in the next verse He says, "Ye shall find rest." Yes, that is another rest, a still deeper one, which you find when you willingly take Christ's yoke upon you and become His disciples, learning of Him. So I do believe my text means just that. God's word is very sweet to the taste when you receive it by faith but it has another and a special and deeper sweetness when you bring it into your mouth, and confess Christ before men.

And let me add to this that there is a very special sweetness about preaching Christ in the public *proclamation* of His word. It may be that some brother here has the gift of speech, but has never used it for his Master. Let me put in my witness here. God's word has been unutterably sweet to my own heart as I have believed it; it has been remarkably precious to me as I have confessed it as a Christian man; but still there is a something, I cannot tell you what, of singular delight about the preaching of this word. Oh, sometimes, when I have prepared my sermon, it has been bitter in my belly, but it has been as honey in my mouth when I have preached it to the great congregation gathered here! If I might choose my destiny, and if I had even to stop out of heaven for the purpose, it would be heaven to me to be permitted always to be preaching Christ and the glories of His salvation; and I do not know that I would have any choice between that and heaven. If I might be privileged to be, without ceasing, lauding and praising and extolling that dear Word of God, the Christ who was born at Bethlehem, if I might tell out to sinners everywhere that God is in Him making reconciliation, no, that He has made reconciliation for all who believe in Him, this might be heaven enough, at least for one poor heart, world without end.

"How sweet are thy words unto my taste! yes, sweeter than honey to my mouth!" Try, brother, whether it will not sweeten your mouth if you begin to preach Christ. Perhaps you have been too quiet and too silent. Get up and speak for Jesus, and see whether the honey does not come into your mouth at once. In the olden time, they pictured the orator with bees buzzing around his lips, storing up the honey that dropped from his sweet utterances. This may be but a fable concerning the human talker; but certainly it is true of the man who preaches Christ, that his lips drop honey, and the more he speaks of his dear Lord and Master, and the less he tries with human eloquence to magnify himself, the more of sacred sweetness shall there be in every word that he utters.

So I think I have accounted for the repetition, have I not? It is no repetition after all; at least, it is no tautology, it is only a right and necessary repetition.

An Examination

And now I am going to wind up, in the fourth place, with an examination, the examination of everybody here present tonight. It is the close of the year, and one may not object to a few personal inquiries at such a time.

The first and chief inquiry is this—Are God's words sweet to me? Is Christ Himself, the Master-Word of God, the *Logos*, is He sweet to me? For, if not, what is the reason?

First, may it be that I have no taste? *Have I spiritual taste?* It would be a sad thing to be wholly without natural taste; I do know one such person who has no taste at all. The poet Wordsworth was for years without the power of smell. His was a very remarkable case, with a mind so dainty, so delicate, so beautiful. Once upon a time, for a very short season, the power of smell came to him among the heather, and you know how every primrose by the river's brim had words for Wordsworth and did talk with him; and when the sweet perfume came from the dear May flowers, the poet was quite enraptured, as if he had for a little while entered into heaven. But the power of smell soon went away, and he was again unhappily bereft of it. The richest flower, the sweetest shrub, could be nothing to the man whose nostril was not sensitive to its perfume.

And what if that should be so with me spiritually? Perhaps, my dear hearer, you have heard all we have been saying about Christ, and you have heard many rich and rare hymns about Him; but you never did feel that there was any sweetness in Him. Then I beg you to inquire whether you may not be lacking in a sense which others have. If a person were to say to me, "How lovely is that Italian sky! What a deep blue it has!" and if I turned my face that way, and said, "I see nothing at all"; if, when he pointed to the sea or to the green fields, I looked in that direction and saw nothing, what should I infer? Why, that he possessed a power called sight, which I did not possess! Of course, I might be foolish enough to say, "There is no blue sky; there is no such thing. There are no green fields; there is no ocean; there is no sun; I am sure there is not, for I never saw them."

One day, I saw a man sitting at a table with his napkin under his chin enjoying his dinner; and he overheard an observation that I made about a sinner, and he said, "I never had a spiritual sensation in my life, and I do not believe that there is anything spiritual in this world." Now, if I had been standing near a sty and a pig had made that observation, I would not have contradicted him; and I did not contradict this man, for I thought that he spoke the truth, I quite believed that he had never experienced a spiritual sensation in his life! And when some men say, "I perceive no sweetness in Christ, and, therefore, there is none," I wish that they would draw another inference, "Therefore I have not that taste which would enable me to perceive His sweetness"; for that is just the truth. A man who has never been born again is dead as to all spiritual things, and he cannot hear or see or taste anything that is spiritual. He is not alive to God as yet. I put this solemn inquiry to every one who says,

"I see no beauty in Christ," may it not be that you have no eyes? If you say, "I hear no music in His voice; in fact, I do not hear that voice," may it not be that your ears are sealed? And if you say, "I taste no sweetness in the word of God, or the Christ of God," may it not be that you are still dead in trespasses and sins? If so, may God quicken you of His infinite mercy!

Still, there is another answer to the question which I beg to put by way of examination. If the word of God be not very sweet to me, *have I an appetite?* Solomon says, "The full soul loatheth an honeycomb; but to the hungry soul every bitter thing is sweet." Ah, when a soul is full of itself, and of the world, and of the pleasures of sin, I do not wonder that it sees no sweetness in Christ, for it has no appetite! Oh, but when a soul is emptied, when a soul hungers and thirsts after God, when it is conscious of its wants and miseries, as I hope some here present are, then is Christ sweet indeed! O hungry ones, take Him into your souls, suck down His precious word! Christ has come on purpose to feed hungry spirits. It you want Him, you may have Him; and the more you want Him, the more free He is to you, and the more freely may you partake of Him. He is just such a Christ as you want. May God make you ravenous after Him, so ravenous that you may never rest until you have received Him as altogether your own!

Yet still there is another answer. If I do not taste sweetness in Christ, *am I in health?* When a man is ill, his soul "abhorreth all manner of meat." Nothing tastes nice to a man whose palate is out of order through sickness. Now, does it happen, tonight, that some of you do not feel any joy in Christ? Then you are ill, brother. Put your tongue out, let us look at it. Ah, it has got furred up with the world, I am sure! Something ails you if Christ is not sweet. Sometimes, you have sat in these pews, some of you, and you have heard Christ preached until you hardly knew how to keep your seats. You have been ready to stand up and clap your hands to the praise of His dear name; and now you do not feel anything at all. You can almost go to sleep, if you do not actually slumber. The preacher is quite willing to share the blame with you, for he is not all he ought to be; but he does not mean to take all the blame of it, for, as far as he knows how, he preaches the same Savior now as ever, and tries to preach Him with as much earnestness as ever. May it not be possible, brother or sister, that you are not quite right spiritually, that you are getting ill, that your heart is growing feeble? Go home, and pray the Lord to set you right. Oh, that He would cleanse you, and purify you, and make you yet to be strong and vigorous; and then this would be one of the first tokens of it, that Christ would once more become inexpressibly sweet to you!

I must also get you to ask yourself this question—*Have I savored the world or sin?* People sometimes lose their appetite for sweetness by eating something sour. You may have had one flavor in your mouth, but when you have eaten something with a different flavor, you cannot taste the first. If a man gets fond of the leeks and the garlic and the onions of Egypt—strong things those—if he once gets the savor of them into his mouth, he is not likely to have any very dainty tooth for the precious things of God. Spiritual flavors have need of great spirituality to enjoy them, I know not what other word to use. They need that the palate be kept clean; for otherwise, if the world is sweet to us, if sin has any hold upon us, to that extent and degree shall we be incapable of appreciating the sweet things of God.

This is my last question—*Have I habituated myself to this food?* All earthly sweetness cloys; he who eats honey for a long while will care no more for honey. But it is very different with the Christ of God. The sweetness of Christ is not fully known except to those who have known Him long, who by reason of constant use have had their senses fully exercised. There is none so greedy after Christ as the man who has had most of Him. Paul had been a believer at least fifteen years, and yet he said this was his ambition, "That I may know him." Had he not known Christ before? Yes; but the more he knew Him, the more he longed to know Him. Come, brother, if you do not taste the sweetness of Christ tonight in the preaching of the word, surely it must be because you have not of late been feeding upon Him. Make haste, and come along; and let your soul be filled with Him, even from this glad hour.

I have done when I have reminded those here present who see no sweetness in the words of God, that there is a time coming when they will be compelled to hear the word of God in a very different way from that in which they hear it tonight. One of the first works of the Resurrection will be the creation of the ear. I do not know by what process we shall be raised from the dead, except that the Lord Jesus said this, "The hour is coming in the which all that are in the graves shall hear his voice, and shall come forth; they that have done good, unto the resurrection of life; and they that have done evil, unto the resurrection of damnation." When the voice of the Son of God shall strike upon that ear of yours, what a sensation it will cause! God has spoken to you now by the voice of one like yourself, and He has spoken according to the printed page; and you have chosen not to hear it; but when, in that last day, He shall speak by the angel's trumpet, and by the voice of His Son, you will be obliged to hear; and rising from your grave, bursting your cerements, you must obey, and you must stand, willing or unwilling, before that last dread tribunal, to answer for every deed done in the body, for every idle word than you have spoken, aye, and for every thought that you have imagined against the Most High

God! It may be a thousand years before that will happen, it may be ten thousand years, I cannot tell; but it will happen in God's time, and that space between will be but as the twinkling of an eye, and there will you be before the face of the great Judge, and you will not be able to say with David, "How sweet are thy words unto my taste!" but, you will cry out, in the agony of your spirit, "Oh, the gall and wormwood!" Oh, the fire that shall burn into your very soul when God shall say, "Because I have called, and ye refused; I have stretched out my hand, and no man regarded; but ye have set at nought all my counsel, and would none of my reproof: I also will laugh at your calamity; I will mock when your fear cometh." "Depart from me ye cursed, into everlasting fire, prepared for the devil and his angels." God grant that you may not be bidden so to depart; and, that you may not, I pray you now to listen to the voice of God, which bids you trust Jesus and live! I can only speak with these poor feeble lips, and there is no power in anything that I can say; but God the Holy Spirit can speak with irresistible might to your hearts, and constrain you to taste of Christ tonight by hearing the word of God in your very soul. I pray that He may do it. for His dear name's sake! Amen and Amen

6

Christic in Gethsemane

And they came to a place which was named Gethsemane (Mark 14:32).

Our Lord had been sitting at the table of happy fellowship with His disciples, talking to them in a very solemn and impressive manner; He then delivered those choice discourses which are recorded by John, and offered that wonderful prayer which deserves ever to be called "*The* Lord's prayer." Knowing all that was to befall Him, He left the Upper Room with His disciples, and started to go to His usual place of quiet retreat, "a place which was named Gethsemane."

You can easily picture their descent into the street. The moon was at the full on the paschal night, and it was very cold, for we read that the high priest's servants' had kindled a fire and warmed themselves because it was cold. As Jesus walked along the narrow streets of Jerusalem, He doubtless still spoke to His disciples in calm and helpful tones, and before long they come to the brook Kedron, over which David passed when Absalom stole away the hearts of the people from his father. So, now, "great David's greater Son" must go the same way to the olive garden where He had often been before with His disciples. It was called Gethsemane, "the olive press." As we think of Christ in Gethsemane, I want you who love Him not only to adore Him, but to learn to imitate Him, so that, when you are called to drink of His cup, and to be baptized with the baptism wherewith He was baptized, you may behave as His true follower's should, and come forth from your conflict victorious as He came forth from His.

At the very outset, there is one fact that I wish you to observe very particularly. Sudden changes from joy to grief have produced extraordi-

This sermon was taken from *The Metropolitan Tabernacle Pulpit* and was preached on Sunday evening, June 1, 1879.

nary results in those who have been affected by them. We have often read or heard of persons whose hair has turned white in a single night; such an extreme convulsion of mind has happened to them that they have seemed to be hurried forward into premature old age, at least in appearance, if not in fact. Many have died through unusual excitements of spirit. Some have dropped down dead through a sudden excess of joy, and others have been killed by a sudden excess of grief. Our blessed Master must have experienced a very sudden change of feeling on that memorable night. In that great intercessory prayer of His, there is nothing like distress or tumult of spirit; it is as calm as a lake unruffled by the zephyr's breath. Yet He is no sooner in Gethsemane than He says to the three specially favored disciples, "My soul is exceeding sorrowful, even unto death: tarry ye here, and watch with me."

I do not think that this great conflict arose through our dear Master's fear of death, nor yet through His fear of the physical pain and all the ignominy and shame that He was so soon to endure. But, surely, the agony in Gethsemane was part of the great burden that was already resting upon Him as His people's Substitute; it was this that pressed His spirit down even into the dust of death. He was to bear the full weight of it upon the cross, but I feel persuaded that the passion began in Gethsemane. You know that Peter writes, "Who his own self bare our sins in his own body on the tree"; but we are not to gather, from that passage, that His substitutionary sufferings were limited to the tree, for the original might bear this rendering—that He bore our sins in His own body up to the tree, that He came up to the tree bearing that awful load, and still continued to bear it on the tree. You remember that Peter also writes, in the same verse, "by whose stripes ye were healed." Those stripes did not fall upon Jesus when He was upon the cross, it was in Pilate's judgment hall that He was so cruelly scourged. I believe that He was bearing our sins all His life, but that the terrible weight of them began to crush Him with sevenfold force when He came to the olive press, and that the entire mass rested upon Him with infinite intensity when He was nailed to the cross, and so forced from Him the agonizing cry, "My God, my God, why hast thou forsaken me?"

The Choice of the Spot

In meditating upon this commencement of our Savior's unknown agonies, let us think, first, of the choice of the spot where those agonies were to be endured. Let us try to find out why He went to that particular garden on that dread night of His betrayal.

First, the choice of Gethsemane *showed His serenity of mind, and His courage.* He knew that He was to be betrayed, to be dragged before Annas and Caiaphas, Pilate and Herod, to be insulted, scourged, and at last to be led away to be crucified; but (mark the words) "he came out, and went, as he was wont, to the Mount of Olives." It was His usual custom to go there to pray, so He would not make any change in His habit although He was approaching the supreme crisis of His earthly life. Let this courageous conduct of our Lord teach a lesson to all who profess to be His disciples. Whenever some trouble is about to come upon you, especially if it is a trouble that comes upon you because you are a Christian, do not get perturbed in spirit. Neglect no duty, but just do as you have been wont to do. The best way of preparing for whatever may be coming is to go on with the next thing in the order of providence. If any child of God knew that he had to die tonight, I would recommend him to do just what he should do on any other Sabbath night, only to do it more earnestly and more devoutly than ever he had done it before.

Blessed is that servant who, when his Master comes, shall be found discharging his duty as a servant, waiting upon his Master's household with all due orderliness and care. To go and stand outside the front door, and stare up into the sky to see if the Master is coming, as some I know seem to do, is not at all as your Lord would have you act. You know how the angels rebuked the disciples for doing this: "Ye men of Galilee, why stand ye gazing up into heaven?" Go and preach the Gospel in the power of the Holy Spirit, and then, whether Christ comes soon or later, you will be in the right posture to welcome Him, and He will commend you for carrying out so far as you can His last great commission to His disciples.

Christ's courage is also evident from the fact that "Judas also, which betrayed Him, knew the place; for Jesus oftentimes resorted thither with his disciples." Nothing would have been easier than for our blessed Lord to have escaped from Judas if He had desired to do so; but He had no desire to escape, so He went boldly and deliberately to the place with which "the son of perdition" was well acquainted, the very place, indeed, to which the traitor at once conducted the officers who had been ordered to arrest the Master. May the Lord give to us similar courage whenever we are placed in a position in any respect like His was then! There are certain trials which, as a Christian, you cannot escape, and which you should not wish to escape. You do not like to think of them, but I would urge you to do so, not with fear and terror, but with the calm confidence of one who says, "I have a baptism to be baptized with, and I am straitened until it is accomplished. I have a cup of which I must drink, I am eager to drink it. I do not court suffering, but if it be for Christ's sake, for the glory of God, and the good of His church, I do not wish to escape from it, but I will go to it calmly and deliberately, even as my Lord went to Gethsemane, though Judas knew the place where Jesus often resorted with His disciples."

But, next, in the choice of this spot, our Lord also *manifested His wisdom*. For, first, it was to Him a place of holy memories. Under those old olive trees, so gnarled and twisted, He had spent many a night in prayer; and the silver moonbeams, glancing between the somber foliage, had often illumined His blessed person as He there knelt, and wrestled, and had communion with His Father. He knew how His soul had been refreshed while He had spoken there face-to-face with the Eternal, how His face had been made to shine, and He had returned to the battle in Jerusalem's streets strengthened by His contact with the Almighty. So He went to the old trysting place, the familiar spot where holy memories clustered thick as bees about a hive, each one laden with honey; He went there because those holy memories aided His faith.

And, brothers and sisters in Christ, when your time of trial comes, you will do well to go to the spot where the Lord has helped you in the past, and where you have enjoyed much hallowed fellowship with Him. There are rooms where, if the walls could tell all that has happened within them, a heavenly brightness might be seen because God has so graciously revealed Himself to us there in times of sickness and sorrow. One, who had long lain in prison for Christ's sake, used sometimes to say, after he had been released, "Oh, take me back to my dungeon, for I never had such blessed seasons of communion with my Lord as I had within that cold stone cell!" Well, if you have such a place, dear to you by many hallowed memories, go to it as your Master went to His sacred oratory in the garden of Gethsemane, for there you will be likely to be helped even by the associations of the place.

Our Lord's wisdom in choosing that spot is also evident from the fact that it was a place of deep solitude, and therefore most suitable for His prayers and cries on that doleful night. The place which is now called the garden of Gethsemane does not, according to some of the best judges, deserve that name. It is in far too exposed a position, and one always thinks of Gethsemane as a very quiet, lonely spot; and let me say that, in my judgment, there is no place so suitable for solitude as an olive garden, especially if it be in terrace above terrace as in the South of France. I have frequently been sitting in an olive garden, and friends, whom I would have been glad to see, have been within a few yards of me, yet I have not known that they were there.

One beautiful afternoon, as two or three of us sat and read, we could see, a long way down, a black hat moving to and fro, but we could not see the wearer of it. We afterward discovered that he was a brother minister whom we were glad to invite to join our little company. If you want to be alone, you can be so at any time you like in an olive garden, even if it is near the town. What with the breaking up of the ground into terraces, and the great abundance of foliage, and the strange twisted trunks of the old trees, I know no place in which I should feel so sure of being quite alone as in an olive garden, and I think our Master went to Gethsemane for a similar reason. A soul burdened as His was needed to be in a solitary place. The clamorous crowds in Jerusalem would have been no fit companions for Him when His soul was exceeding sorrowful, even to death.

It seems to me, also, that there is about an olive garden, either by day or by night, something congruous with sorrow. There are some trees that seem conducive to mirth, the very twinkling of their leaves would make one's heart dance with delight; but about the olive there is always something, not suggestive, perhaps, of absolute melancholy, but a matter-of-fact soberness as if, in extracting oil out of the flinty rock, it had endured so much suffering that it had no inclination to smile, but stood there as the picture of everything that is somber and solemn. Our dear Master knew that there was something congenial to His exceeding sorrow in the gloom of the olive garden, and therefore He went there on the night of His betrayal. Act with similar wisdom, brothers and sisters in Christ, when your hour of trial is approaching. I have known some people rush into happy society to try to forget their grief; but that was folly. I have known others, in seasons of sorrow, seek to surround themselves with everything that is sad; that also was folly. Some, who have been in great trouble, have tried to hide it in frivolity; but that was still greater folly. It is a good thing, in times of grief, not to let your surroundings be either too somber or too bright; but to seek, in your measure, to be as wise as your Master was in His choice of Gethsemane as the scene of His solitary supplication and subsequent betrayal.

The Exercise of the Savior upon That Spot

Now, secondly, let us consider the exercise of the Savior upon that spot. Every item is worthy of attention and imitation.

First, *He took all due precautions for others.* He left eight of His disciples at the entrance to the garden, saying to them, "Pray that ye enter not into temptation." Then He took Peter, and James, and John a little further into the garden, saying to them, "Tarry ye here, and watch with me." There ought thus to have been two watching and praying bands. If they had all been on the watch, they might have heard the footfalls of the approaching band, and they would have seen in the distance the lights of the lanterns and torches of those who were coming to arrest their Lord. Probably our Master took these precautions more for the sake of His disciples than for His own sake. He bade them pray as well as watch, that they might not be taken unawares, nor be overcome with fear when they saw their Master captured, and led away as a prisoner. From this action of our Lord, we may learn that we also, in our own extremity, should not forget to care for others, and shield them from harm so far as we can.

Next, *our Savior solicited the sympathy of friends.* As a man, He desired the prayers and sympathies of those who had been most closely associated with Him. Oh, what a prayer meeting they might have held—watching for the coming of the enemy, and praying for their dear Lord and Master! They had a noble opportunity of showing their devotion to Him, but they missed it. They could not have kept Judas, and the men who came with Him, away from their Lord; but they might have let their Master know when Judas was coming. It was almost the last service that any of them could have rendered to Him before He died for them; yet they failed to render it, and left Him, in that dread hour of darkness, without even the slight consolation that human sympathy might have afforded Him. In our times of trial, we shall not do wrong if we imitate our Lord in this action of His; yet we need not be surprised if, like Him, we find all human aid fail us in our hour of greatest need.

Then, leaving all His disciples, and going away alone, *Jesus prayed and wrestled with God*; and, in our time of trouble, our resort must be to prayer. Restrain not prayer at any time, even when the sun shines brightly upon you; but be sure that you pray when the midnight darkness surrounds your spirit. Prayer is most needed in such an hour as that, so be not slack in it, but pour out your whole soul in earnest supplication to your God, and say to yourself, "Now above all other times I must pray with the utmost intensity." For consider how Jesus prayed in Gethsemane.

He adopted the lowliest posture and manner. "He fell on his face, and prayed, saying, O my Father, if it be possible, let this cup pass from me." What an extraordinary sight! The eternal Son of God had taken upon Himself our nature, and there He lay as low as the very dust out of which our nature was originally formed. There He lay as low as the most unrighteous sinner or the humblest beggar can lie before God. Then He began to cry to His Father in plain and simple language; but, oh! what force He put into the words He used! Thrice He pleaded with His Father, repeating the same petition; and Luke tells us that, "being in an agony he prayed more earnestly; and his sweat was as it were great drops of blood falling down to the ground." He was not only in an agony of suffering, but in an agony of prayer at the same time.

But while our Lord's prayer in Gethsemane was thus earnest, and intense, and repeated, it was at the same time balanced with a ready acquiescence in His Father's will: "Nevertheless not as I will, but as thou wilt." So, suffering one, thou whose spirit has sunk within thee, thou who art depressed and well-nigh distracted with grief, may the Holy Spirit help thee to do what Jesus did—to pray, to pray alone, to pray with intensity, to pray with importunity, to pray even unto an agony, for this is the way in which you will prevail with God, and be brought through your hour of darkness and grief. Believe not the Devil when he tells you that your prayer is in vain. Let not your unbelief say, "The Lord hath closed his ear against thee." "Behold, the Lord's hand is not shortened, that it cannot save; neither his ear heavy, that it cannot hear." Yet mind that you do also imitate your Lord's submission and resignation, for that is not acceptable prayer in which a man seeks to make his own will prevail over the will of God. That is presumption and rebellion, and not the cry of a true child of God. You may beseech Him to grant your request "if it be possible," but you may not go beyond that, but must still cry, with your Lord, "Nevertheless not as I will, but as thou wilt."

I have already reminded you that our Lord sought human sympathy while in Gethsemane, but I want again to refer to that fact so that we may learn the lessons it is intended to teach us. In our little griefs, we often go to our fellow creatures, but not to God; that habit is apt to breed dependence upon man. But, in our greater griefs, we frequently go to God, and feel as if we could not go to man. Now, although that may look like honoring God, there is a good deal of pride mixed with it. Our Lord Jesus Christ neither depended upon men nor yet renounced the sympathy of men. There were three of His disciples within call, and eight more a little further away, but still probably within call. He prayed to His Father, yet He asked of His disciples such sympathy as they might have shown to Him. Still, He did not depend upon their sympathy; for, when He did not get it, He went back to His praying to His Father. There are some who say that they will trust in God, and use no means; others say that they will use the means, but they fall short in the matter of trusting God.

I have read that one of Muhammad's followers came to him, and said, "O prophet of God, I shall turn my camel loose tonight, and trust it to providence"; but Muhammad very wisely answered, "Tie your camel up as securely as you can, and then trust it to providence." There was sound common sense in that remark, and the principle underlying it can be applied to far weightier matters. I believe that I am following the example of my Lord when I say, "I trust in God so fully that, if no man will sympathize with me, He alone will enable me to drink all that is in this cup that He has placed in my hand; yet I love my fellow creatures so much that I desire to have their sympathy with me in my sorrow; although, if they withhold it, I shall still place my sole dependence upon my God."

When our Lord came to His disciples, and found them sleeping instead of watching, you know how prompt He was to find an excuse for them: "The spirit truly is ready, but the flesh is weak." His rebuke of Peter was very gentle: "Simon, sleepest thou? couldest not thou watch one hour?" Art *thou* sleeping, thou who so recently boasted that thou wouldst go with Me to prison and to death, and that, though all others should deny Me, thou wouldst not? Ah, Simon! thou hadst better watch and pray, for thou knowest not how soon temptation may assail thee, and cause thee to fall most grievously. Yet Peter was included with the rest of the disciples in the excuse which their Lord made for the willing but weak sleepers who ought to have been watchers. What a lesson this is to us! We do not make half the excuses for one another that Jesus makes for us. Generally, we are so busy making excuses for ourselves that we quite forget to make excuses for others. It was not so with our Lord. Even in His own overwhelming trouble, no sharp or unkind word escaped from His lips. When we are very ill, you know how apt we are to be irritable to those about us; and if others do not sympathize with us as we think they should, we wonder what they can be made of to see us in such sorrow, and not to express more grief on our account. Yet there was our Master, all bestained with His own blood, for His heart's floods had burst their banks, and run all over Him in a gory torrent; but when He came to His disciples, they gave Him no kind word, no help, no sympathy, for they were all asleep. He knew that they were sleeping for sorrow; so their sleep was not caused by indifference to His grief, but by their sorrow at His sorrow. Their Master knew this, so He made such excuse for them as He could; and, beloved, when we are suffering our much smaller sorrows, let us be ready to make excuses for others as our Lord did in His great ocean sufferings.

The Triumph upon That Spot

Now, thirdly, let us consider the triumph upon that spot. It was a terrible battle that was waged in Gethsemane—we shall never be able to pronounce that word without thinking of our Lord's grief and agony— but it was a battle that He won, a conflict that ended in complete victory for Him.

The victory consisted, first, *in His perfect resignation*. There was no rebellion in His heart against the will of the Father to whom He had so completely subjected Himself; but unreservedly He cried, "Not as I will, but as thou wilt." No clarion blast, nor firing of cannon, nor waving of flags, nor acclamation of the multitudes ever announced such a victory as our Lord achieved in Gethsemane. He there won the victory over all the griefs that were upon Him, and all the griefs that were soon to roll over Him, like huge Atlantic billows. He there won the victory over death, and over even the wrath of God which He was about to endure to the utmost for His people's sake. There is true courage, there is the highest heroism, there is the declaration of the invincible Conqueror in that cry "Not as I will, but as thou wilt."

With Christ's perfect resignation, there was also *His strong resolve.* He had undertaken the work of His people's redemption, and He would go through with it until He could triumphantly cry from the cross, "It is finished." A man can sometimes dash forward and do a deed of extraordinary daring, but it is the long-sustained agony that is the real test of courageous endurance. Christ's agony in Gethsemane was broken up into three periods of most intense wrestling in prayer, with brief intervals which can have given Him no relief as He turned in vain to the sleeping disciples for the sympathy that His true human nature needed in that hour of dreadful darkness. But, as He had before steadfastly set His face to go to Jerusalem, though He well knew all that awaited Him there, He still kept His face set like a flint toward the great purpose for which He had come from heaven to earth. It is the wear and tear of long-continued grief that has proved too much for many a truly heroic spirit, yet our Lord endured it to the end, and so left us an example that we shall do well to follow.

A part of our Savior's victory was that *He obtained angelic help.* Those prayers of His prevailed with His Father, "and there appeared an angel unto him from heaven, strengthening him." I know not how He did it, but in some mysterious way the angel brought Him succor from on high. We do not know that angel's name, and we do not need to know it; but somewhere among the bright spirits before the throne, there is the angel who strengthened Christ in Gethsemane. What a high honor for him! The disciples missed the opportunity that Christ put within their reach, but the angel gladly availed himself of the opportunity as soon as it was presented to him.

Last of all, the victory of Christ was manifest in *His majestic bearing toward His enemies.* Calmly He rose, and faced the hostile band; and when the traitor gave the appointed signal by which Jesus was to be recognized, He simply asked the searching personal question, "Judas, betrayest thou the Son of man with a kiss?" How that inquiry must have cut the betrayer to the heart! When Jesus turned to those who had been sent to arrest Him, and said to them, "Whom seek ye?" He did not speak like a man whose soul was exceeding sorrowful, even to death; and when they answered Him, "Jesus of Nazareth," He said, "I am," and at the very sound of that great Jehovah-name, "I AM," "they went backward, and fell to the ground."

There was a majestic flash of His deity even in the hour of the abasement of His humanity, and they fell prostrate before the God who had thus confessed that the name of Jehovah rightly belonged to Him. Then He went with them quietly, and without the slightest resistance, after He had shown His care for His disciples by saying, "If therefore ye seek me, let these go their way"; and after He had healed the ear of Malchus, which Peter had so rashly cut off. Then, all the while that Christ was before Annas and Caiaphas, and before Pilate and Herod, and right on to the last dread scene of all upon the cross, He was calm and collected, and never again endured such tossings to and fro as He had passed through in Gethsemane.

Well now, beloved, if the Lord shall bring us into deep waters, and cause us to pass through fiery trials, if His Spirit shall enable us to pray as Jesus did, we shall see something like the same result in our own experience. We shall rise up from our knees strengthened for all that lies before us, and fitted to bear the cross that our Lord may have ordained for us. In any case, our cup can never be as deep or as bitter as was His, and there were in His cup some ingredients that never will be found in ours. The bitterness of sin was there, but He has taken that away for all who believe in Him. His Father's wrath was there, but He drank that all up, and left not a single dreg for any one of His people.

One of the martyrs, as he was on his way to the stake, was so supremely happy that a friend said to him, "Your Savior was full of sorrow when He agonized for you in Gethsemane." "Yes," replied the martyr, "and for that very reason I am so happy, for He bore all the sorrow for me." You need not fear to die if you are a Christian, since Jesus died to put away your sin, and death is but the opening of your cage to let you fly, to build your happy nest on high. Therefore, fear not even the last enemy, which is death. Besides, Christ could not have a Savior with Him to help Him in His agony, but you have His assurance that He will be with you. You shall not have merely an angel to strengthen you, but you shall have that great Angel of the covenant to save and bless you even to the end.

The most of this sermon does not belong to some of you, for you do not belong to Christ. O dear friends, do not give sleep to your eyes or slumber to your eyelids until you do belong to Him! As surely as you live, you will have sorrows at some time or other, you will have a bitter cup of which you must drink, and then what will you do if you have no divine consolation in the trying hour! What will you do especially when you come to die if you have no Christ to make your pillow soft for you, no Savior to go with you through that dark valley? Oh, seek Him, and He will be found of you, even now! The Lord help you to do so for Christ's sake! Amen.

7
The Betrayal

*And while he yet spake, behold a multitude, and he that was called
Judas, one of the twelve, went before them, and drew near unto
Jesus to kiss him. But Jesus said unto him, Judas, betrayest thou the
Son of man with a kiss? (Luke 22:47–48).*

When Satan had been entirely worsted in his conflict with
Christ in the garden, the man-devil Judas came upon the
scene. As the Parthian in his flight turns around to shoot the
fatal arrow, so the archenemy aimed another shaft at the Redeemer, by
employing the traitor into whom he had entered. Judas became the
Devil's deputy, and a most trusty and serviceable tool he was. The Evil
One had taken entire possession of the apostate's heart, and, like the
swine possessed of devils he ran violently downward toward destruction. Well had infernal malice selected the Savior's trusted friend to be
His treacherous betrayer, for thus He stabbed at the very center of His
broken and bleeding heart.

But, beloved, as in all things God is wiser than Satan, and the Lord
of goodness outwits the Prince of Evil, so, in this dastardly betrayal of
Christ, prophecy was fulfilled, and Christ was the more surely declared
to be the promised Messiah. Was not Joseph a type? and, lo! like that
envied youth, Jesus was sold by His own brethren. Was He not to be
another Samson, by whose strength the gates of hell should be torn
from their posts? lo! like Samson, He is bound by His countrymen and
delivered to the adversary. Do you not know that He was the antitype of
David? and was not David deserted by Ahithophel, his own familiar
friend and counselor? No, brethren, do not the words of the psalmist receive a literal fulfillment in our Master's betrayal? What prophecy can
be more exactly true than the language of Psalm 41 and 55? In Psalm

---

This sermon was taken from *The Metropolitan Tabernacle Pulpit* and was
preached on Sunday morning, February 15, 1863.

41 we read, "Yea, mine own familiar friend in whom I trusted, which did eat of my bread, hath lifted up his heel against me"; and in Psalm 55 the psalmist is yet more clear, "For it was not an enemy that reproached me; then I could have borne it: neither was it he that hated me that did magnify himself against me; then I would have hid myself from him: but it was thou, a man mine equal, my guide, and mine acquaintance. We took sweet counsel together, and walked unto the house of God in company. He hath put forth his hands against such as be at peace with him: he hath broken his covenant. The words of his mouth were smoother than butter, but war was in his heart: his words were softer than oil, yet were they drawn swords."

Even an obscure passage in one of the lesser prophets must have a literal fulfillment, and for thirty pieces of silver, the price of a base slave, must the Savior be betrayed by His choice friend. Ah! you foul fiend, you shall find at the last that your wisdom is but intensified folly; as for the deep plots and plans of your craft, the Lord shall laugh them to scorn; after all, you are but the unconscious drudge of Him whom you abhor; in all the black work you do so greedily, you are no better than a mean scullion in the royal kitchen of the King of Kings.

Without further preface, let us advance to the subject of our Lord's betrayal. First, concentrate your thoughts upon *Jesus, the betrayed one*; and when you have lingered awhile there, solemnly gaze into the villainous countenance of *Judas, the betrayer*—he may prove a beacon to warn us against the sin which genders apostasy.

Jesus, the Betrayed One

It is appointed that He must die, but how shall He fall into the hands of His adversaries? Shall they capture Him in conflict? It must not be, lest He appear an unwilling victim. Shall He flee before His foes until He can hide no longer? It is not meet that a sacrifice should be hunted to death. Shall He offer Himself to the foe? That were to excuse His murderers, or be a party to their crime. Shall He be taken accidentally or unawares? That would withdraw from His cup the necessary bitterness which made it wormwood mingled with gall. No; He must be betrayed by His friend, that He may bear the utmost depths of suffering, and that in every separate circumstance there may be a well of grief! One reason for the appointment of the betrayal lay in the fact *that it was ordained that man's sin should reach its culminating point in His death.* God, the great owner of the vineyard, had sent many servants, and the husbandmen had stoned one and cast out another; last of all, He said, "I will send my Son; surely they will reverence my Son." When they slew the heir to win the inheritance, their rebellion had reached its height. The murder of our blessed Lord was the extreme of human guilt; it developed the deadly hatred against God which lurks in the heart of man. When man became a deicide, sin had reached its fullness; and in the black deed of the man by whom the Lord was betrayed, that fullness was all displayed. If it had not been for a Judas, we would not have known how black, how foul, human nature may become.

I scorn the men who try to apologize for the treachery of this devil in human form, this son of perdition, this foul apostate. I should think myself a villain if I tried to screen him, and I shudder for the men who dare extenuate his crimes. My brethren, we should feel a deep detestation of this master of infamy; he has gone to his own place, and the anathema of David, part of which was quoted by Peter, has come upon him, "When he shall be judged let him be condemned: and let his prayer become sin. Let his days be few; and let another take his office." Surely, as the Devil was allowed unusually to torment the bodies of men, even so was he let loose to get possession of Judas as he has seldom gained possession of any other man, that we might see how foul, how desperately evil is the human heart.

Beyond a doubt, however, the main reason for this was *that Christ might offer a perfect atonement for sin*. We may usually read the sin in the punishment. Man betrayed his God. Man had the custody of the royal garden, and should have kept its green avenues sacred for communion with his God; but he betrayed the trust; the sentinel was false; he admitted evil into his own heart, and so into the paradise of God. He was false to the good name of the Creator, tolerating the insinuation which he should have repelled with scorn. Therefore must Jesus find man a traitor to Him. There must be the counterpart of the sin in the suffering which He endured. You and I have often betrayed Christ. We have, when tempted, chosen the evil and forsaken the good; we have taken the bribes of hell, and have not followed closely with Jesus. It seemed most fitting, then, that He who bore the chastisement of sin should be reminded of its ingratitude and treachery by the things which He suffered.

Besides, brethren, that *cup must be bitter to the last degree which is to be the equivalent for the wrath of God*. There must be nothing consolatory in it; pains must be taken to pour into it all that even Divine wisdom can invent of awful and unheard of woe, and this one point—"He that eateth bread with me hath lifted up his heel against me," was absolutely necessary to intensify the bitterness.

Moreover, we feel persuaded that by thus suffering at the hand of a traitor *the Lord became a faithful High Priest*, able to sympathize with us when we fall under the like affliction. Since slander and ingratitude are common calamities, we can come to Jesus with full assurance of faith; He knows these sore temptations, for He has felt them in their very worst degree. We may cast every care, and every sorrow upon Him, for He cares for us, having suffered with us. Thus, then, in our Lord's betrayal, Scripture was fulfilled, sin was developed, atonement was completed, and the great all-suffering High Priest became able to sympathize with us in every point.

Now let us *look at the treason itself*. You perceive how black it was.

Judas was *Christ's servant*, what if I call him His confidential servant. He was a partaker in apostolic ministry and the honor of miraculous gifts. He had been most kindly and indulgently treated. He was a sharer in all the goods of his Master, in fact he fared far better than his Lord, for the Man of Sorrows always took the lion's share of all the pains of poverty and the reproach of slander. He had food and raiment given him out of the common stock, and the Master seems to have indulged him very greatly. The old tradition is, that next to the apostle Peter he was the one with whom the Savior most commonly associated. We think there must be a mistake there, for surely John was the Savior's greatest friend; but Judas, as a servant, had been treated with the utmost confidence. You know, brethren, how sore is that blow which comes from a servant in whom we have put unlimited trust.

But Judas was more than this: *he was a friend, a trusted friend.* That little bag into which generous women cast their small contributions had been put into his hands, and very wisely too, for he had the financial vein. His main virtue was economy, a very needful quality in a treasurer. As exercising a prudent foresight for the little company, and watching the expenses carefully, he was, as far as men could judge, the right man in the right place. He had been thoroughly trusted. I read not that there was any annual audit of his accounts; I do not discover that the Master took him to task as to the expenditure of his privy purse. Everything was given to him, and he gave, at the Master's direction, to the poor, but no account was asked. This is vile indeed, to be chosen to such a position, to be installed purse-bearer to the King of Kings, Chancellor of God's exchequer, and then to turn aside and sell the Savior; this is treason in its uttermost degree.

Remember that the world looked upon Judas *as colleague* and partner with our Lord. To a great extent the name of Judas was associated with that of Christ. When Peter, James, or John had done anything amiss, reproachful tongues threw it all on their Master. The Twelve were part and parcel of Jesus of Nazareth. One old commentator says of Judas—"He was Christ's alter ego"—to the people at large there was an identification of each apostle with the leader of the band. And oh! when such associations have been established, and then there is treachery, it is as though arm should commit treason against head, or as if foot should desert the body. This was a stab indeed!

Perhaps, dear brethren, our Lord saw in the person of Judas *a representative man*, the portraiture of the many thousands who in after ages imitated his crime. Did Jesus see in Iscariot all the Judases who betray truth, virtue, and the cross? Did He perceive the multitudes of whom we may say that they were, spiritually, in the loins of Judas? Hymeneus, Alexander, Hermogenes, Philetus, Demas, and others of that tribe, were all before Him as He saw the man, His equal, His acquaintance, bartering Him away for thirty pieces of silver.

Dear friends, the position of Judas must have tended greatly to aggravate his treason. Even the heathens have taught us that ingratitude is the worst of vices. When Caesar was stabbed by his friend Brutus, the world's poet writes—

> This was the most unkindest cut of all;
> For when the noble Caesar saw him stab,
> Ingratitude, more strong than traitor's arms,
> Quite vanquish'd him; then burst his mighty heart;
> And, in his mantle muffling up his face,
> Even at the base of Pompey's statue,
> > great Caesar fell.

Many ancient stories, both Greek and Roman, we might quote to show the abhorrence which the heathens entertain toward ingratitude and treachery. Certain, also, of their own poets, such, for instance, as Sophocles, have poured out burning words upon deceitful friends; but we have no time to prove what you will all admit, that nothing can be more cruel, nothing more full of anguish than to be sold to destruction by one's bosom friend. The closer the foeman comes the deeper will be the stab he gives; if we admit him to our hearts and give him our closest intimacy, then can he wound us in the most vital part.

Let us notice, dear friends, while we look at the breaking heart of our agonizing Savior, *the manner in which He met this affliction.* He had been much in prayer; prayer had overcome His dreadful agitation; He was very calm; and we need to be very calm when we are forsaken by a friend. Observe His gentleness. The first word He spoke to Judas, when the traitor had polluted His cheek with a kiss, was this— "FRIEND!" FRIEND! Note that! Not "Thou hateful miscreant," but "Friend, wherefore art thou come?" not "Wretch, wherefore dost thou dare to stain my cheek with thy foul and lying lips?" no, "Friend, wherefore art thou come?" Ah! if there had been anything good left in Judas, this would have brought it out. If he had not been an unmitigated, incorrigible, thrice-dyed traitor, his avarice must have lost its power at that instant, and he would have cried—"My master! I came to betray You, but that generous word has won my soul; here, if Thou must be bound, I will be bound with You; I make a full confession of my infamy!" Our Lord added these words—there is reproof in them, but notice how kind they are still, how much too good for such a caitiff—"Judas, betrayest thou the Son of Man with a kiss?" I can conceive that the tears gushed from His eyes, and that His voice faltered, when He thus addressed His own familiar friend and acquaintance—"Betrayest *thou*," My Judas, My treasurer, "betrayest thou *the Son of Man*," your suffering, sorrowing friend, whom you have seen naked and poor, and without a place whereon to lay His head. Betray you *the Son of Man*—and do you prostitute the fondest of all endearing signs—*a kiss*—that which should be a symbol of loyalty to the King, shall it be the badge of your treachery—that which was reserved for affection as her best symbol—do you make it the instrument of My destruction? Do you betray the Son of Man with a kiss?

Oh! if he had not been given up to hardness of heart, if the Holy Spirit had not utterly left him, surely this son of perdition would have fallen prostrate yet again, and weeping out his very soul, would have cried—"No, I cannot betray You, suffering Son of Man; forgive, forgive; spare Yourself; escape from this bloodthirsty crew, and pardon Your treacherous disciple!" But no, no word of compunction, while the silver is at stake! Afterward came the sorrow that works death, which drove him, like Ahithophel, his prototype, to court the gallows to escape remorse. This, also, must have aggravated the woe of our beloved Lord, when He saw the final impenitence of the traitor, and read the fearful doom of that man of whom He had once said, it would be better for him that he had never been born.

Beloved, I would have you fix your eyes on your Lord in your quiet meditations as being thus despised and rejected of men, a man of sorrows and acquainted with grief; and gird up the loins of your minds, counting it no strange thing if this fiery trial should come upon you, but being determined that though your Lord should be betrayed by His most eminent disciples, yet, through His grace you will cling to Him in shame and in suffering, and will follow Him, if needs be, even to death. God give us grace to see the vision of His nailed hands and feet, and remembering that all this came from the treachery of a friend, let us be very jealous of ourselves, lest we crucify the Lord afresh and put Him to an open shame by betraying Him in our conduct, or in our words, or in our thoughts.

Judas, the Betrayer

I would call your attention, dear friends, *to his position and public character*. Judas was *a preacher*; no, he was a foremost preacher, "he obtained part of this ministry," said the apostle Peter. He was not simply one of the seventy; he had been selected by the Lord Himself as one of the Twelve, an honorable member of the college of the apostles. Doubtless he had preached the Gospel so that many had been gladdened by his voice, and miraculous powers had been vouchsafed to him, so that at his word the sick had been healed, deaf ears had been opened, and the blind had been made to see; no, there is no doubt that he who could not keep the Devil out of himself had cast devils out of others. Yet how are you fallen from heaven, O Lucifer, son of the morning! He that was as a prophet in the midst of the people, and spoke with the tongue of the learned, whose word and wonders proved that he had been with Jesus and had learned of Him—he betrays his Master.

Understand, my brethren, that no gifts can ensure grace, and that no position of honor or usefulness in the church will necessarily prove our being true to our Lord and Master. Doubtless there are bishops in hell, and crowds of those who once occupied the pulpit are now condemned forever to bewail their hypocrisy. You that are church officers, do not conclude that because you enjoy the confidence of the church, that therefore of an absolute certainty the grace of God is in you. Perhaps it is the most dangerous of all positions for a man to become well known and much respected by the religious world, and yet to be rotten at the core. To be where others can observe our faults is a healthy thing though painful; but to live with beloved friends who would not believe it possible for us to do wrong, and who if they saw us err would make excuses for us—this is to be where it is next to impossible for us ever to be aroused if our hearts be not right with God. To have a fair reputation and a false heart is to stand upon the brink of hell.

Judas *took a very high degree officially*. He had the distinguished honor of being entrusted with the Master's financial concerns, and this, after all, was no small degree to which to attain. The Lord, who knows how to use all sorts of gifts, perceived what gift the man had. He knew that Peter's unthinking impetuosity would soon empty the bag and leave the company in great straits, and if he had entrusted it to John, his loving spirit might have been cajoled into unwise benevolence toward beggars of unctuous tongue; he might even have spent the little moneys in buying alabaster boxes whose precious ointments should anoint the Master's head. He gave the bag to Judas, and it was discreetly, prudently, and properly used; there is no doubt he was the most judicious person, and fitted to occupy the post. But oh! dear friends, if the Master shall choose any of us who are ministers or church officers, and give us a very distinguished position; if our place in the ranks shall be that of commanding officers, so that even our brother ministers look up to us with esteem, and our fellow elders or deacons regard us as being fathers in Israel—oh! if we turn, if we prove false, how damnable shall be our end at the last! What a blow shall we give to the heart of the church, and what derision will be made in hell!

You will observe that the character of Judas *was openly an admirable one.* I find not that he committed himself in any way. Not the slightest speck defiled his moral character so far as others could perceive. He was no boaster, like Peter; he was free enough from the rashness which cries, "Though all men should forsake thee yet will not I." He asks no place on the right hand of the throne, his ambition is of another sort. He does not ask idle questions. The Judas who asks questions is "not Iscariot." Thomas and Philip are often prying into deep matters, but not Judas. He receives truth as it is taught him, and when others are offended and walk no more with Jesus, he faithfully adheres to Him, having golden reasons for so doing. He does not indulge in the lusts of the flesh or in the pride of life. None of the disciples suspected him of hypocrisy; they said at the table, "Lord, is it I?" They never said, "Lord, is it Judas?"

It was true he had been filching for months, but then he did it by little, and covered his defalcations so well by financial manipulations that he ran no risk of detection from the honest unsuspecting fishermen with whom he associated. Like some merchants and traders we have heard of—invaluable gentlemen as chairmen of speculating companies and general managers of swindling banks—he could abstract a decent percentage and yet make the accounts exactly tally. The gentlemen who have learned of Judas manage to cook the accounts most admirably for the shareholders, so as to get a rich joint for their own table—over which they, no doubt, entreat the divine blessing. Judas was, in his known life, a most admirable person. He would have been an alderman before long there is no doubt, and being very pious and richly gifted, his advent at churches or chapels would have created intense satisfaction. "What a discreet and influential person"; say the deacons. "Yes," replies the minister; "what an acquisition to our councils; if we could elect him to office he would be of eminent service to the church."

I believe that the Master chose him as an apostle on purpose that we might not be at all surprised if we find such a man a minister in the pulpit, or a colleague of the minister, working as an officer in Christ's church. These are solemn things, my brethren; let us take them to heart, and if any of us wear a good character among men and stand high in office, let this question come home close to us—"Lord, is it I?" Perhaps he who shall last ask the question is just the man who ought to have asked it first.

But, secondly, I call your attention *to his real nature and sin.* Judas was a man with a conscience. He could not afford to do without it. He was no Sadducee who could fling religion overboard; he had strong religious tendencies. He was no debauched person; he never spent a twopence in vice on his life, not that he loved vice less, but that he loved the twopence more. Occasionally he was generous, but then it was with other people's money. Well did he watch his lovely charge, the bag. He had a conscience, I say, and a ferocious conscience it was when it once broke the chain, for it was his conscience which made him hang himself. But then it was a conscience that did not sit regularly on the throne; it reined by fits and starts.

Conscience was not the leading element. Avarice predominated over conscience. He would get money, if honestly, he liked that best, but if he could not get it conscientiously, then anyhow in the world. He was but a small trader; his gains were no great things or else he would not have sold Christ for so small a sum as that—ten pounds at the outside, of our money at its present value—some three or four pounds, as it was in those days. It was a poor price to take for the Master; but then a little money was a great thing to him. He had been poor; he had joined Christ with the idea that He would soon be proclaimed King of the Jews, and that then he should become a nobleman and be rich.

Finding Christ a long while in coming to His kingdom, he had taken little by little, enough to lay by in store; and now, fearing that he was to be disappointed in all his dreams, and never having had any care for Christ, but only for himself, he gets out of what he thinks to have been a gross mistake in the best way he can, and makes money by his treason against his Lord.

Brethren, I do solemnly believe, that of all hypocrites, those are the persons of whom there is the least hope whose God is their money. You may reclaim a drunkard; thank God, we have seen many instances of that; and even a fallen Christian, who has given way to vice, may loathe his lust, and return from it; but I fear me that the cases in which a man who is cankered with covetousness has ever been saved, are so few, that they might be written on your fingernail. This is a sin which the world does not rebuke; the most faithful minister can scarce smite its forehead. God knows what thunders I have launched out against men who are all for this world, and yet pretend to be Christ's followers; but yet they always say, "It is not for me."

What I would call stark naked covetousness, they call prudence, discretion, economy, and so on; and actions which I would scorn to spit upon, they will do, and think their hands quite clean after they have done them, and still sit as God's people sit, and hear as God's people hear, and think that after they have sold Christ for paltry gain, they will go to heaven. O souls, souls, souls, beware, beware, beware, most of all of greed! It is not money, nor the lack of money, but *the love* of money which is the root of all evil. It is not getting it; it is not even keeping it;

it is loving it; it is making it your god; it is looking at that as the main chance, and not considering the cause of Christ, nor the holy life of Christ, but being ready to sacrifice everything for gains' sake. Oh! such men make giants in sin; they shall be set up forever as butts for infernal laughter; their damnation shall be sure and just.

The third point is, *the warning which Judas received, and the way in which he persevered.* Just think—the night before he sold his Master what do you think the Master did? Why, He washed his feet! And yet he sold Him! Such condescension! Such love! Such familiarity! He took a towel, and girded Himself, and washed Judas's feet! And yet those very feet brought Judas as a guide to them that took Jesus! And you remember what He said when He had washed his feet—"Now ye are clean, but not all"; and He turned a tearful eye on Judas.

What a warning for him! What could be more explicit? Then when the supper came, and they began to eat and drink together, the Lord said—"One of you shall betray me." That was plain enough; and a little farther on He said explicitly—"He that dippeth with me in the dish the same is he." What opportunities for repentance! He cannot say he had not a faithful preacher. What could have been more personal? If he does not repent now, what is to be done? Moreover, Judas saw that which was enough to make a heart of adamant bleed; he saw Christ with agony on His face, for it was just after Christ had said, "Now is my soul troubled," that Judas left the feast and went out to sell his Master. That face, so full of grief, ought to have turned him, must have turned him, if he had not been given up and left alone, to deliver over his soul to his own devices. What language could have been more thundering than the words of Jesus Christ, when He said, "Woe unto that man by whom the Son of man is betrayed; it had been good for that man if he had not been born." He had said, "Have not I chosen you twelve, and one of you is a devil."

Now, if while these thunders rolled over his head, and the lightning flashes pointed at his person, if, then, this man was not aroused, what a hell of infernal pertinacity and guilt must have been within his soul! Oh! but if any of you, if any of you shall sell Christ for the sake of keeping the shop open on Sunday, if you shall sell Christ for the extra wages you may earn for falsehood—oh! if you shall sell Christ for the sake of the hundred pounds that you may lay hold of by a villainous contract—if you do that, you do not perish unwarned. I come into this pulpit to please no man among you. God knows if I knew more of your follies you should have them pointed out yet more plainly; if I knew more of the tricks of business, I would not flinch to speak of them! But, O sirs, I do conjure you by the blood of Judas, who hanged himself at last, turn you—if such there be—turn you from this evil, if haply your sin may be blotted out!

Let us for one minute *notice the act itself*. He sought out his own temptation. He did not wait for the Devil to come to him; he went after the Devil. He went to the chief priests and said, "What will ye give me?" One of the old Puritan divines says, "This is not the way people generally trade; they tell their own price." Judas says, "What will you give me?" Anything you like. The Lord of life and glory sold at the buyer's own price. What will you give me? And another very prettily puts it, "What could they give him? What did the man want? He did not want food and raiment; he fared as well as his Master and the other disciples; he had enough; he had all that his needs could crave, and yet he said, What will you give me? What will you give me? What will you give me?"

Alas! some people's religion is grounded on that one question— "What will you give me?" Yes, they would go to church if there are any charities given away there, but if there were more to be gotten by not going they would do that. "What will you give me?" Some of these people are not even so wise as Judas. Ah! there is a man over yonder who would sell the Lord for a crown, much more for ten pounds, as Judas did! Why there are some who will sell Christ for the smallest piece of silver in our currency. They are tempted to deny their Lord, tempted to act in an unhallowed way, though the gains are so paltry that a year's worth of them would not come to much. No subject could be more dreadful than this. If we really would but look at it carefully, this temptation happens to each of us.

Do not deny it. We all like to gain; it is but natural that we should; the propensity to acquire is in every mind, and under lawful restrictions it is not an improper propensity; but when it comes into conflict with our allegiance to our Master, and in a world like this it often will, we must overcome it or perish. There will arise occasions with some of you many times in a week in which it is "God—or gain"; "Christ, or the thirty pieces of silver"; and therefore I am the more urgent in pressing this on you.

Do not, though the world should bid its highest, though it should heap its comforts upon one another, and add fame, and honor, and respect, do not, I pray you, forsake your Master. There have been such cases; cases of persons who used to come here, but they found they did not get on, because Sunday was the best day's trade in the week; they had some good feelings, some good impressions once, but they have lost them now. We have known others who have said, "Well, you see, I did once think I loved the Lord, but my business went so badly when I came up to the house of God, that I left it; I renounced my profession." Ah, Judas! ah, Judas! ah, Judas! let me call you by your name, for such you are! This is the sin of the apostate over again; God help you to repent of it, and go, not to any priest, but to Christ and make confession, if haply you may be saved.

You perceive that in the act of selling Christ, Judas was faithful to his master. "Faithful to his master?" you say. Yes, his master was the Devil, and having made an agreement with him he carried it out honestly. Some people are always very honest with the Devil. If they say they will do a wrong thing they say they ought to do it because *they said* they would; as if any oath could be binding on a man if it be an oath to do wrong? "I will never go into that house again," some have said, and they have said afterward, "Well, I wish I had not said it." Was it a wrong thing? What is your oath then? It was an oath given to the Devil. What was that foolish promise but a promise to Satan, and will you be faithful to him? Ah! would God that you were faithful to Christ! Would that any of us were as true to Christ as Satan's servants are to their master!

Judas betrayed his Master with a kiss. That is how most apostates do it; it is always with a kiss. Did you ever read an infidel book in your life which did not begin with profound respect for truth? I never have. Even modern ones, when bishops write them, always begin like that. They betray the Son of Man with a kiss. Did you ever read a book of bitter controversy which did not begin with such a sickly lot of humility, such sugar, such butter, such treacle, such everything sweet and soft, that you said, "Ah! there is sure to be something bad here, for when people begin so softly and sweetly, so humbly and so smoothly, depend upon it they have rank hatred in their hearts." The most devout looking people are often the most hypocritical in the world.

We conclude with *the repentance of Judas*. He did repent; he did repent; but it was the repentance that works death. He did make a confession, but there was no respect to the deed itself, but only to its consequences. He was very sorry that Christ was condemned. Some latent love that he had once had to a kind Master came up when he saw that He was condemned. He did not think, perhaps, it would come to that; he may have had a hope that He would escape out of their hands, and then he would keep his thirty pieces of silver, and perhaps sell Him over again. Perhaps he thought that He would rid Himself from their hands by some miraculous display of power, or would proclaim the kingdom, and so he himself would only be hastening on that very blessed consummation.

Friends, the man who repents of consequences does not repent. The ruffian repents of the gallows but not of the murder, and that is no repentance at all. Human law of course must measure sin by consequences, but God's law does not. There is a pointsman on a railway who neglects his duty; there is a collision on the line, and people are killed; well, it is manslaughter to this man through his carelessness.

That pointsman, perhaps, many times before had neglected his duty, but no accident came of it, and then he walked home and said, "Well, I have done no wrong." Now the wrong, mark you, is never to be measured by the accident, but by the thing itself, and if you have committed an offense and you have escaped undetected it is just as vile in God's eye; if you have done wrong and providence has prevented the natural result of the wrong, the honor of that is with God, but you are as guilty as if your sin had been carried out to its fullest consequences, and the whole world set ablaze. Never measure sin by consequences, but repent of them as they are in themselves.

Though being sorry for consequences, since these are unalterable, this man was led to remorse. He sought a tree, adjusted the rope, and hanged himself, but in his haste he hanged himself so badly that the rope broke, he fell over a precipice, and there we read his bowels gushed out; he lay a mangled mass at the bottom of the cliff, the horror of every one who passed. Now you that make a gain of godliness—if there be such here—you may not come to a suicide's end, but take the lesson home.

Mr. Keach, my venerable predecessor, gives at the end of one of his volumes of sermons, the death of a Mr. John Child. John Child had been a Dissenting minister, and for the sake of gain, to get a living, he joined the Episcopalians against his conscience; he sprinkled infants, and practiced all the other paraphernalia of the church against his conscience. At last, at last, he was arrested with such terrors for having done what he had, that he renounced his living, took to a sickbed, and his dying oaths, and blasphemies, and curses, were something so dreadful, that his case was the wonder of that age. Mr. Keach wrote a full account of it, and many went to try what they could do to comfort the man, but he would say, "Get ye hence; get ye hence; it is of no use; I have sold Christ."

You know, also, the wonderful death of Francis Spira. In all literature, there is nothing so awful as the death of Spira. The man had known the truth; he stood well among reformers; he was an honored, and to a certain extent apparently a faithful man; but he went back to the church of Rome; he apostatized; and then when conscience was aroused he did not fly to Christ, but he looked at the consequences instead of at the sin, and so, feeling that the consequences could not be altered, he forgot that the sin might be pardoned, and perished in agonies extreme.

May it never be the unhappy lot of any of us to stand by such a deathbed; but the Lord have mercy upon us now, and make us search our hearts. Those of you who say, "We do not want that sermon," are probably the persons who need it most. He who shall say, "Well, we have no Judas among us," is probably a Judas himself. Oh! search yourselves; turn out every cranny; look in every corner of your souls, to see whether your religion be for Christ's sake, and for truth's sake, and for God's sake, or whether it be a profession which you take up because it is a respectable thing, a profession which you keep up because it keeps you up. The Lord search us and try us, and bring us to know our ways.

And now, in conclusion—there is a Savior, and that Savior is willing to receive us now. If I am not a saint, yet I am a sinner. Would it not be best for all of us to go again to the fountain, and wash and be clean. Let each of us go anew, and say, "Master, You know what I am; I know not myself; but, if I be wrong, make me right; if I be right, keep me so. My trust is in You. Keep me now, for Your own sake, Jesus." Amen.

8

Our Lord's Trial Before the Sanhedrin

And they all condemned him to be guilty of death (Mark 14:64).

This one sentence is selected because custom demands a text; but in reality we shall follow the entire narrative of our Lord's trial before the high priests. We shall see how the Sanhedrim arrived at their unrighteous sentence, and what they did afterward, and so, in a sense, we shall be keeping to our text. We have just been reading three passages—John 23:12–24; Mark 14:53–65; and Luke 22:66–71. Please to carry these in your minds while I rehearse the mournful story.

The narrative of our Lord's grief, if it be carefully studied, is harrowing in the extreme. One cannot long think of it without tears; in fact, I have personally known what it is to be compelled to leave my meditations upon it from excess of emotion. It is enough to make one's heart break fully to realize the sufferings of such an One, so lovely in Himself and so loving toward us. Yet this harrowing of the feelings is exceedingly useful: the after result of it is truly admirable. After mourning for Jesus we are raised above our own mourning. There is no consolation under heaven at all like it; for the sorrows of Christ seem to take the sting out of our own sorrows, until they become harmless and endurable. A sympathetic contemplation of our Lord's grief so dwarfs our griefs that they are reckoned to be but light afflictions, too petty, too insignificant, to be mentioned in the same day. We dare not write ourselves down in the list of the sorrowful at all when we have just seen the sharp pains of the Man of Sorrows. The wounds of Jesus distill a balm which heals all mortal ills.

This sermon was taken from *The Metropolitan Tabernacle Pulpit* and was preached on Sunday morning, February 5, 1882.

95

Nor is this all, though that were much in a world of woe like this; but there is a matchless stimulus about the passion of the Lord. Though you have been almost crushed by the sight of your Lord's agonies, you have risen therefrom strong, resolute, fervent, consecrated. Nothing stirs our hearts' depths like His heart's anguish. Nothing is too hard for us to attempt or to endure for One who sacrificed Himself for us. To be reviled for His dear sake who suffered such shame for us becomes no great affliction; even reproach itself when borne for Him becomes greater riches than all the treasures of Egypt. To suffer in body and in mind, even to death, for Him were rather a privilege than an exaction. Such love so swells our hearts that we vehemently pant for some way of expressing our indebtedness. We are grieved to think that our best will be so little; but we are solemnly resolved to give nothing less than our best to Him who loved us and gave Himself for us.

I believe also that full often careless hearts have been greatly affected by the sufferings of Jesus; they have been disturbed in their indifference, convinced of their ingratitude, weaned from their love of sin, and attracted to Christ by hearing what He bore on their behalf. No loadstone can draw human hearts like the Cross of Christ. His wounds cause even hearts of stone to bleed. His shame makes obstinacy itself ashamed. Men never so plentifully fall before the great bow of God as when its arrows are dipped in the blood of Jesus. Those darts which are armed with His agonies cause wounds such as never can be healed except by His own pierced hands. These are the weapons which slay the sin and save the sinner killing at one stroke both his self-confidence and his despair, and leaving him a captive to that conqueror whose glory it is to make men free.

This morning I would not only preach the doctrines that come on of the Cross, but the Cross itself. I suppose that was one of the great differences between the first preaching of all and the preaching after the Reformation. After the Reformation we had clearly ringing out from all pulpits the doctrine of justification by faith and other glorious truths, which I hope will be made more and more prominent; but the first fathers of the church set forth the same truths in a less theological fashion. If they dwell little upon justification by faith they were wonderfully full upon the blood and its cleansing power, the wounds and their healing efficacy, the death of Jesus and our eternal life. We will go back to their style for awhile, and preach the facts about our Lord Jesus Christ rather than the doctrinal inferences therefrom. Oh, that the Holy Spirit would so bring the sorrows of our Lord near to each heart that every one of us may know the fellowship of His sufferings, and possess faith in His salvation and reverent love for His person.

The Preliminary Examination

We will begin our narrative this morning by first asking you to think of the preliminary examination of our blessed Lord and Master by the high priest. They brought in our Lord from the garden bound; but they also kept fast hold upon Him, for we read of "the men that held him." They were evidently afraid of their prisoner, even when they had Him entirely in their power. He was all gentleness and submission; but conscience made cowards of them all, and they therefore took all a coward's care to hold Him in their grasp. As the court had not yet gathered in sufficient numbers for a general examination, the high priest resolved that he would fill up the time by personally interrogating his prisoner.

He commenced his malicious exercise. The high priest asked Jesus *concerning His disciples.* We cannot tell what were the questions, but I suppose they were something like these: "How is it that Thou hast gathered about Thee a band of men? What did they with Thee? What was Thine ultimate intention to do by their means? Who were they? Were they not a set of fanatics, or men discontented and ready for sedition?" I do not know how the crafty Caiaphas put his questions; but the Savior gave no reply to this particular inquiry. What could He have said if He had attempted to answer? Ah, brothers, what good could He have said of His disciples? We may be sure He would say no ill. He might have said, "Concerning My disciples, one of them has betrayed Me; he has still the blood money in his hand which you gave him as My price. Another of them, down in the hall there, before the cock crows will deny that he ever knew Me, and add oaths and cursing to his denial; and as for the rest, they have all forsaken Me and fled." Therefore our Lord said nothing concerning His disciples, for He will not turn the accuser of His own, whom He came, not to condemn, but to justify.

The high priest also asked Him concerning *His doctrine.* I suppose he said to Him, "What new teaching is this of Yours? Are we not sufficient to teach the people—the scribes so learned in the law, the Pharisees so attentive to ritual, the Sadducees so philosophical and speculative? Why do You need intrude into this domain? I suppose You to be little more than a peasant's son; what is this strange teaching of Yours?"

To this inquiry our Lord did answer, and what a *triumphant reply* it was! Oh, that we could always speak, when it is right to speak, as meekly and as wisely as He! He said, "I spake openly to the world; I ever taught in the synagogue and in the temple, whither the Jews always resort, and in secret I have said nothing. Why askest thou me? ask them which heard me what I have said unto them: behold, they know what I have said." Oh, brethren, no reply to slander can be compared with a blameless life. Jesus had lived in the full blaze of day where all could see, and yet He was able to challenge accusation and say, "Ask them which heard me." Happy is the man who has no need to defend himself because his works and words are solid testimonials to his uprightness and goodness. Our Savior answered His questioner very gently, but yet most effectually, by His appeal to facts. He stands before us at once the mirror of meekness and the paragon of perfection, with slander like a wounded snake writhing at His feet. What a delight to have this triumphant Pleader for our advocate, to urge His own righteousness in our defense! None can impugn His absolute perfection, and that perfection covers all His saints this day. Who shall accuse us now that Jesus has undertaken to plead for us?

This overwhelming answer, however, brought the Savior *a blow from one of the officers of the court* who stood by. Was not this a most shocking deed? Here was the first of a new order of assaults. Hitherto we have not heard of strokes and blows; but now it is fulfilled, "They shall smite the Judge of Israel with a rod upon his cheek." This was the first of a long series of assaults. I wonder who the man was that struck the Master so. I could wish that the Master's reply to him may have influenced his heart to repentance; but if not, it is certain that he led the van in personal assaults upon our Lord's person: his impious hand first struck Him. Surely if he died in impenitence the memory of that blow must remain as a never-dying worm within him. Today he cried, "I was the first to smite Him; I struck Him on the mouth the palm of my hand."

The old writers upon the Passion give us various details of the injuries inflicted upon the Savior by that blow; but we attach no importance to such traditions, and therefore will not repeat them, but simply say that there was general belief in the church that this blow was a very grievous one, and caused the Savior much pain. Yet while He felt that blow, and was perhaps half staggered by it, the Master did not lose His composure, or exhibit the least resentment. His reply was everything it ought to be. There is not a word too much. He does not say, "God shall smite thee, thou whited wall," as did the apostle Paul. We will not censure the servant, but we will far more commend the Master. He meekly said, "If I have spoken evil, bear witness of the evil: but if well, why smitest thou me?" Enough, surely, if there remained any tenderness in the heart of the aggressor, to have made him turn his hand upon his own breast in penitential grief. One would not have wondered had he cried out, "Forgive me, O You divinely meek and gentle One, and let me henceforth be Your disciple."

Thus have we seen the first part of our Lord's sufferings in the house of the high priest, and the lesson from it is just this—Let us be meek and lowly in heart as the Savior was, for herein lay His strength and dignity.

You tell me I have said that before. Yes, brethren, and I shall have to say it several more times before you and I have learned the lesson well. It is hard to be meek when falsely accused, meek when roughly interrogated, meek when a cunning adversary is on the catch, meek when smarting under a cruel blow which was a disgrace to a court of justice. You have heard of the patience of Job, but it pales before the patience of Jesus. Admire His forbearance, but do not stop at admiration; copy His example, write under this headline and follow every stroke. O Spirit of God, even with Christ for an example, we shall not learn meekness unless You teach us; and even with You for a teacher we shall not learn it unless we take His yoke upon us and learn of Him; for it is only at His feet, and under Your divine anointing that we shall ever become meek and lowly of heart, and so find rest to our souls.

The preliminary examination is therefore over, and it has ended in no success whatever for the high priest. He has questioned Jesus and he has smitten Him, but the ordeal brings nothing to content the adversary. The Prisoner is supremely victorious, the assailant is baffled.

The Search for Witnesses Against Him

Now comes a second scene, the search for witnesses against Him. "The chief priests and all the council sought for witness against Jesus to put Him to death; and found none." A strange court that meets with the design to find the prisoner guilty, resolved in some way or other to compass His death. They must proceed according to the forms of justice, and so they summon witnesses, though all the while they violate the spirit of justice, for they ransack Jerusalem to find witnesses who will perjure themselves to accuse the Lord. Every man of the council is writing down somebody's name who may be fetched in from the outside, for the people have come from all parts of the land to keep the Passover, and surely some may be hunted up who, in one place or another, have heard Him use an actionable mode of speech. They fetch in, therefore, everyone that they can find of that degraded class who will venture upon perjuring themselves if the bribe be forthcoming.

They scour Jerusalem to bring forth witnesses against Jesus but they had great difficulty in accomplishing their design, because they were bound to examine the witnesses apart, and they could not make them agree. Lies cannot be easily made to pair with each other, whereas truths are cut to the same pattern. Moreover, many sorts of witnesses that they could readily find they did not dare to bring forward. Witnesses were forthcoming who could testify that Jesus had spoken against the tradition of the elders; but in that some who were in the council, namely, the Sadducees, were agreed with Him to a large extent, it would never do to bring forward a charge about which they would not be unanimous. His denunciations of the Pharisees could not be the charge, for these pleased the Sadducees; neither could they allege His outcry against the Sadducees for in this the Pharisees were agreed with Him. You recollect how Paul, when brought before this Sanhedrin, took advantage of their division of opinion and cried, "I am a Pharisee, the son of a Pharisee; of the hope and resurrection of the dead I am called in question"; and in this manner created a dissension among the conclave, which for a time wrought in his favor. Our Lord took higher and nobler ground, and did not stoop to turn their folly to His own benefit; yet, they being conscious of their internal feuds, cautiously avoided those points upon which they were not in harmony.

They might have brought forward their old grievance that the Lord Jesus did not observe the Sabbath after their fashion; but then it would have come out more publicly that He had healed the sick on the Sabbath. It would not do to publish that fact, for who would think of putting a person to death for having opened the eyes of one born blind, or having restored a withered arm on the Sabbath day? That kind of witness was therefore set aside. But might they not have found some witnesses to swear that He had talked about a kingdom that He was setting up? Might not this readily have been made to mean sedition and rebellion? Yes, but then that was rather a charge to allege against Him before Pilate's civil court, whereas theirs was an ecclesiastical tribunal. Moreover, there were Herodians in the council who were very restive under the Roman yoke, and could not have had the face to condemn anyone for being a patriot and beside, the people outside would have sympathized with Jesus all the more if they had supposed that He would lead them on rebelling against Caesar. Therefore they could not urge that point.

They must have been greatly puzzled to know what to do, especially when even on those points which they decided to bring forward the witnesses no sooner opened their mouths than they contradicted each other. At last they had it. There came two whose evidence was somewhat agreed; they asserted that on a certain occasion Jesus Christ had said, "I will destroy this temple that is made with hands, and within three days I will build another made without hands." Here was blasphemy against the holy and beautiful house of the Lord, and this would serve their turn. Now, the Savior had said something which was a little like the testimony of these false witnesses, and a misunderstanding had made it more like it; but still their statement was a lie, and nonetheless a lie because a shadow of truth had fallen upon it, for the worst kind of lie is that which is manufactured out of a truth: it does more mischief a great deal than if it were a falsehood from stem to stern.

The Savior had not said, "I will destroy this temple"; He said "Destroy this temple," that is to say, "Ye will destroy it, and ye may destroy it." He had not referred to the Jerusalem temple at all; this spoke He concerning the temple of His body which would be destroyed. Christ has never said, "Destroy this temple which is made with hands, and I will build another without hands"; in His language there is no allusion to hands at all. These refinements were of their own inventing, and His language gave no cover for them. He had not said, "I will build another"; He had said, "I will raise it up," which is quite a different thing. He meant that His body, after being destroyed, would be raised up again on the third day. They had altered a word here and a word there, the mood of one verb and the form of another, and so they made out our Lord to say what He never thought of. Yet even on that charge they did not agree. One said one thing upon it, and another said another, so that even this paltry accusation could not be brought against the Savior. Their patched-up falsehood was made of such rotten stuff that the pieces would not hold together. They were ready to swear to anything that came into their perjured imaginations, but they could not be gotten to swear any two of them to the selfsame thing.

Meanwhile the Lord Himself *stands silent*; like the sheep before her shearers, He is dumb, and opens not His mouth; and I suppose the reason was partly that He might fulfill the prophecy, partly because the grandeur of His soul could not stoop to contend with liars, and most of all because His innocence needed no defense. He that is in some measure guilty is eager to apologize and to extenuate; His excuses usually suggest to men of experience the belief that there may be some to answer His slanderers, for they soon answer one another. Our Lord did not desire to get into a vain jangle with them, and so to lead them on to utter still more falsehoods. If speech can do not good then indeed silence is wise; when the only result would have been to provoke His enemies to add to their iniquities it was magnanimous compassion which led the slandered Savior to hold His speech.

We must not refrain from noticing *the comfort* which in some degree had been ministered to our Lord by the accusation which came most to the front. He stands there, and He knows they are about to put Him to death, but they themselves remind Him that their power over Him has no longer lease than three days, and at the end of that short time He will be raised up again, no more to be at their disposal. His enemies witnessed the resurrection to Him. I say not that His memory was weak, or that He would possibly have forgotten it amid His sorrows, but yet our Lord was human, and modes of comfort which are valuable to us were also useful to Him. When the mind is tortured with malicious falsehood, and the whole man is tossed about by pains and griefs, it is good for us to be reminded of the consolations of God. We read of some who were "tortured, not accepting deliverance," and it was the hope of resurrection which sustained them. Our Lord knew that His soul would not be left in the abodes of the dead, neither should His flesh see corruption, and the false witnesses brought this vividly before His mind. Now, indeed, could our Redeemer say, "Destroy this temple, and in three days I will raise it up." These ravens have brought the Savior bread and meat. In these dead lions our glorious Samson has found honey. Sustained by the joy that was set before Him He despises the shame. Strange that out of the mouths of those who sought His blood there should come the memorial of one of His greatest glories.

Now, brethren, here again we learn the same lesson as before, namely, let us gain meekness, and prove it by our power to hold our tongues. Eloquence is difficult to acquire, but silence is far more hard to practice. A man may much sooner learn to speak well than learn not to speak at all. We are in such a hurry to vindicate our own cause that we damage it by rash speech. If we were calm, gentle, quiet, forbearing as the Savior was, our pathway to victory would be much more easy.

Observe, again, the armor with which Christ was clad: see the invulnerable shield of His holiness. His life was such that slander could not frame an accusation against Him which would last long enough to be repeated. So frail were the charges that, like bubbles, they vanished as soon as they saw the light. Our Lord's enemies were utterly baffled. They hurled their darts against Him, but, as if they fell upon a shield of blazing diamond, every arrow was broken and consumed.

Learn also this other lesson: that we must expect to be misrepresented; we may reckon that our words will have other meanings to ungracious ears than those which we intended; we may expect that when we teach one thing which is true they will make us out to have stated another which is false; but let us not be overwhelmed by this fiery trial as though it were some strange thing. Our Lord and Master has endured it, and the servants must not escape. Wherefore endure hardness as good soldiers of Jesus Christ, and be not afraid.

Amid the din of these lies and perjuries, I hear the still small voice of a truth most precious, for like as Jesus stood for us at the bar, and they could not cause an accusation to abide upon Him, so when we shall stand in Him at the last great day, washed in His blood and covered with His righteousness, we too shall be clear. "Who shall lay anything to the charge of God's elect?" If Satan should appear as the accuser of the brethren, he will be met by the voice, "The Lord rebuke thee, O Satan, even the Lord that hath chosen Jerusalem rebuke thee: is not this a brand plucked out of the burning?" Yes, beloved, we too shall be cleared of slander. Then shall the righteous shine forth as the sun in the kingdom of their Father. The glorious righteousness of Him who was falsely accused shall deliver the saints and all iniquity shall stop her mouth.

The Personal Interrogation

But I must not dwell too long even on such themes as these, and therefore I pass on to the personal interrogation which followed upon the failure to bring forward witnesses. The high priest, too indignant to sit still, rises and stands over the prisoner like a lion roaring over his prey, and begins to question Him again. It was an unrighteous thing to do. Should the judge who sits to administer law set himself to prove the prisoner guilty, or, what is worse, shall he try to extort confession from the accused which may be used against him? It was a tacit confession that Christ had been proved innocent up until then. The high priest would not have needed to draw something out of the accused one if there had been sufficient material against Him elsewhere. The trial had been a dead failure up to that point, and he knew it, and was red with rage. Now he attempts to bully the Prisoner, that he may extract some declaration from Him which may save all further trouble of witnesses, and end the matter. The question was forced home by a solemn adjuration, and it effected its purpose, for the Lord Jesus did speak, though He knew that He was thereby furnishing a weapon against Himself. He felt under bond to answer the high priest of His people when he used such adjuration, bad man as that high priest was; and He could not draw back from a charge so solemn lest He should seem by His silence to deny the truth upon which the salvation of the world is made to hinge. So when the high priest said to Him, "Art thou the Christ, the Son of the Blessed?" how distinctly and outspoken was the Master's reply. Though He knew that His death would thus be compassed, He witnessed a good confession. He plainly said, "I am," and then He added to that declaration, "Ye shall see the Son of man"—so He brings out His humanity as well as His deity—"sitting on the right hand of power, and coming in the clouds of heaven." What a majestic faith!

It is wonderful to think that He should be so calm as to confront His mockers, and assert His glory while He was in the depths of shame. He did as good as say, "You sit as my judges, but I shall soon sit as your judge: I seem to you to be an insignificant peasant, but I am the Son of the Blessed; you think that you will crush Me, but you never will; for I shall speedily sit at the right hand of the power of God, and come in the clouds of heaven." He speaks boldly, as well became Him. I admire the meekness that could be silent, I admire the meekness that could speak gently, but I still more wonder at the meekness that could speak courageously, and still be meek. Somehow or other, when we rouse ourselves to courage, we let in harshness at the same door, or if we shut out our anger we are very apt to forget our firmness. Jesus never slays one virtue to make room for another. His character is complete, full-orbed, perfect, whichever way we look at it.

And surely, brethren, this must have brought another sweet consolation to our divine Master's heart. While smarting under that cruel blow, while writhing under those filthy accusations, while enduring such contradiction of sinners against Himself, He must have felt satisfied from within in the consciousness of His Sonship and His power, and in the prospect of His glory and triumph. A well of water springs up within His soul as He foresees that He shall sit at the right hand of God, and the He shall judge the living and the dead, and vindicate His redeemed. It is a wise thing to have these consolations always ready to hand. The enemy may not see their consolatory power, but we see it. To us from beneath the altar there issues forth a stream whose gentle flow supplies our spirits with a quiet gladness such as all earth's waters can never rival. Even now we also hear the Father say, "I am thy shield and thy exceeding great reward."

Notice, before we pass away from this point, that, practically, the trial and the interrogation ended in our Lord's being *condemned because of His avowal of His deity*. They said, "Ye have heard the blasphemy: what think ye? And they all condemned him to be guilty of death." I cannot make out at all those people who call themselves Unitarians, and deny our Lord's deity. Unitarians we also are, for we believe in one God, and one God only; but they tell us that this blessed Christ our Master is not God, and yet they own that He was the most excellent of men, the most perfect of human beings. I cannot see it myself. He seems to me to be a blasphemer, and nothing else, if He be not God; and the Jews evidently held that opinion, and treated Him accordingly. If He had not said that God was His Father, they would not have been so enraged against Him. They put Him to death because of the assertion of His deity, and the declaration that He would sit at the right hand of power and judge the world. Today multitudes are willing to take Christ as a teacher, but they will not have Him as the Son of God. I do not doubt that the Christ religion might be received in many places if it were shorn of its strength; of, in fact, its very soul and nothing more. Hear how our wise men talk of Him as one of a line of great reformers, such as Moses, Samuel, Elijah, and they often add Confucius and Muhammad. Do we give place to this? No, not for an instant. He is verily the Son of the Blessed. He is divine, or false. The accusation of blasphemy must lie against Him if He be not the Son of the Highest.

The Condemnation

We must now pass on and linger for a second or two over the condemnation. They condemned Him out of His own mouth: but this, while it wore the semblance of justice, was really unjust. The Prisoner at the bar has affirmed that He is the Son of God. What next? May He not speak the truth? If it be the truth He must not be condemned, but adored. Justice requires that an inquiry be made as to whether He be the Christ, the Son of the Blessed, or not. He has claimed to be the Messiah. Very well, all those in the court are expecting the Messiah; some of them expect Him to appear very speedily. May not this be the sent one of the Lord? Let an inquiry be made into His claims. What is His lineage? Where was He born? Have any prophets attested Him? Has He wrought miracles? Some such inquiries are due to any man whose life is at stake. You cannot justly condemn a man to die without examining into the truth of His defense, for it may turn out that His statements are correct. But, no, they will not hear the man they hate, the mere claim condemns Him; it is blasphemy, and He must die.

He says He is the Son of God. Come, then, Caiaphas and council, call for witnesses for the defense. Inquire whether blind eyes have been opened and the dead raised up. Ask whether He has wrought miracles such as no man ever wrought in the midst of Israel throughout all time. Why not do this? O no, He must be taken from prison and from judgment, and none shall declare His generation. The less inquiry the more easy to condemn Him unjustly, He has said He is the Christ and the Son of God, He is therefore guilty of death. Alas, how many there are who condemn Christ's doctrine without making due inquiries into it—condemn it on the most trivial grounds. They come to hear a sermon, and perhaps find fault with the mannerism of the preacher, as if that were sufficient reason for denying the truth which he preaches; or else they say, "This is so strange—we cannot believe it." Why not? Are not strange things sometimes true, and is not many a truth wondrously strange until you get familiar with it? These men will not condescend to hear Christ's proof of claim, they will make no inquiry. In this, like the Jewish priests, they practically cry, "Away with him! Away with him!"

He is condemned to die, and the high priest rends his clothes. I do not know whether he wore at that time the robes in which he ministered, but doubtless he wore some garb peculiar to his sacerdotal office, and this he rent. Oh, how significant! The house of Aaron and the tribe of Levi had their garments rent, and the temple, within a few hours, rent its veil from the top to the bottom: for priests and temple were

alike abolished. They little knew it, but in all they did there was a singular significance: those rent garments were an index of the fact that
now the Aaronic priesthood was forever rent, and the great Melchisidec
priesthood had come in, for the true Melchisidec there and then stood
before them in all majesty of His patience.

Observe that they were all agreed; there were no dissentients; they
had taken care, I have no doubt, not to let Nicodemus and Joseph of
Arimathea know anything about this meeting of theirs. They held it in
the night, and they only rehearsed it in the early morning, for the sake
of keeping their old rabbinical law that they must try prisoners by daylight. They hurried up the trial, and any that might have spoken against
their bloodthirsty sentence were kept out of the way. The assembly was
unanimous. Alas for the unanimity of ungodly hearts against Christ! It
is wonderful that there should be such quarrels among Christ's friends,
and such unity among His foes, when the point is to put Him to death. I
never heard of quarrels among devils, nor did I ever read of sects in
hell: they are all one in their hatred of the Christ and of God. But here
are we split up into sections and parties, and often at war with one another. O Lord of love, forgive us: King of concord, come and reign over
us, and bring us into a perfect unity around Yourself.

The sentence was "death." I say nothing of it but this. Death was the
sentence due to me, the sentence due to you, and they laid it upon our
Substitute. "Worthy of death"—they said—all of them. All hands were
held up; all voices said "Yea, yea" to the verdict. Yet there was no fault
in Him. Say rather, there was every excellence in Him. As I hear Jesus
condemned to die my soul falls at His feet and cries, "Blessed Lord,
now have You taken my condemnation; there is therefore, none for me.
Now have You taken my cup of death to drink, and henceforth it is dry
to me. Glory be to Your blessed name, henceforth and forever."

The Abuse

I am almost glad that my time is so far advanced, for I must needs
set before you the fifth and most painful scene. No sooner have these
evil men of the Sanhedrim pronounced Him guilty of death, than the
servants, the guards, and those that kept the high priest's hall, eager to
please their masters, and all touched with the same brutelike spirit
which was in them, straightway began to *abuse* the infinite majesty of
our Lord. Consider the abuse. Let me read the words: "Some began to
spit on him." Began to spit on him! Thus was contempt expressed more
effectively than by words. Be astonished, O heavens, and be horribly
afraid. His face is the light of the universe, His person is the glory of
heaven, and they "began to spit on him!" Alas, my God, that man
should be so base! Some went further, and they "covered his face." It is

an Eastern custom to cover the face of the condemned, as if they were not fit to see the light, nor fit to behold their fellowmen. I know not whether for this reason, or in pure mockery, they covered His face, so that they could not see it, and He could not see them. How could they thus put out the sun and shut up bliss. Then when all was dark to Him we read that they began to say, "Prophesy, Who is he that smote thee?" Then another did the like, and many were the cruel cuffs they laid about His blessed face. The medieval writers delighted to talk about the teeth that were broken, the bruises on the cheeks, the blood which flowed, the flesh that bruised and blackened; but we dare not thus imagine. Scripture has cast a veil, and there let it abide. Yet is must have been an awful sight to see the Lord of glory with His face bestained by their accursed phlegm and ridicule of His prophetic claims and dishonor to His divine person. Nothing was thought bad enough. They invented all they could of shame and scorn, and He stood patient there though a single flash of His eye would have consumed them in a moment.

Brothers, sisters, this is what our sin deserved. A shameful thing are you, O sin! You do deserve to be spit upon! This is what sin is constantly doing to Christ. Whenever you and I sin we do, as it were, spit in His face; we also hide His eyes by trying to forget that He sees us; and we also smite Him whenever we transgress and grieve His Spirit. Talk not of cruel Jews; let us think of ourselves, and let us be humbled by the thought. This is what the ungodly world is ever doing to our blessed Master. They also would hide His eyes which are the light of the world; they also despise His Gospel, and spit upon it as an utterly worn-out and worthless thing: they also do despite to the members of His body through His poor afflicted saints who have to bear slander and abuse for His dear sake.

And yet over all this I seem to see a light most blessed. Christ must be spit upon, for He has taken our sin; Christ must be tortured, for He is standing in our stead. Who is to be the executioner of all this grief? Who shall take upon himself the office of putting Christ to shame? Our redemption was being wrought out this way—who shall be the drudge to perform this miserable work? Fling in the clusters richer than the grapes of Eshcol; fling them in, but who shall tread them out and laboriously extract the wine, the generous wine which cheers God and man? The feet shall be the willing feet of Christ's own adversaries; they shall extort from Him that which shall redeem us and destroy all evil. I rejoice to see Satan outwitted, and his malice made to be the means of his own overthrow. He thinks to destroy Christ, and by that deed he destroys himself. He pulls down evil upon his own head and falls into the pit which he has digged. Thus shall all evil ever work for the good of the Lord's people; yes, their greatest good shall oftentimes come out of that which threatened their ruin, and wrought in them the utmost anguish. Three days must the Christ suffer and die and lie in the grave, but after that He must bruise the serpent's head and lead the captivity captive, and that by the means of the very suffering and shame which He is now enduring. In like manner shall it happen to His mystical body, and Satan shall be bruised under our feet shortly.

I leave this subject, hoping that you will pursue it in your meditations. Here are three observations.

First, how ready should we be to bear slander and ridicule for Jesus' sake. Do not get into a huff and think it a hard thing that people should mock at you. Who are you, dear sir? Who are you? What can you be if compared with Christ? If they spat upon Him, why should they not buffet you? Shall your Master have all the rough of it? Shall He have all the bitter, and you all the sweet? A pretty soldier you, to demand better fare than your Captain!

How earnestly, next, ought we to honor our dear Lord. If men were so eager to put Him to shame, let us be ten times more earnest to bring Him glory. Is there anything we can do today by which He may be honored? Let us set about it. Can we make any sacrifice? Can we perform any difficult task which would glorify Him? Let us not deliberate, but at once do it with our might. Let us be inventive in modes of glorifying Him, even as His adversaries were ingenious in the methods of His shame.

Lastly, how surely and how sweetly may all who believe in Him come and rest their souls in His hands. Surely I know that He who suffered this, since He was verily the Son of the Blessed, must have ability to save us. Such griefs must be a full atonement for our transgressions. Glory to God, that spittle on His countenance means a clear, bright face for me. Those false accusations on His character mean no condemnation for me. That putting Him to death proves the certainty of our text last Sabbath morning, "Verily, verily, I say unto you, he that believeth on me hath everlasting life." Let us sweetly rest in Jesus, and if ever our faith is agitated, let us get away to the hall of Caiaphas, and see the Just standing for the unjust, the Faultless One bearing condemnation for sinners. Let us in the high priest's hall judge and condemn every sin and every doubt, and come forth glorying that the Christ has conquered for us, and that we now wait for His appearing with delight. God bless you, brothers and sisters, for Christ's sake. Amen.

9

The King of the Jews

And Pilate wrote a title, and put in on the cross. And the writing was, JESUS OF NAZARETH THE KING OF THE JEWS (John 19:19).

It was the usual custom of the Romans, when a man was put to death by crucifixion, to affix to the cross, somewhere where it might be read, an account of his life. His name and title would be given, and the accusation that had been brought against him, so that all who passed by might read the reason why he had been put to such an ignominious death. Our Savior, therefore, being numbered with the transgressors, must be treated in all respects as they were. If their accusations were published, so must He have His accusation published among the sons of men. How wondrous was the condescension that He, whom all heaven adored as the ever-blessed Son of the Highest, should be hanged upon a tree, and that He should have His accusation written up over His head just as if He had been a common malefactor.

I wish we could realize both the dignity of His person and the shame to which He was exposed. If we could realize this we would be filled with grief for Him, and with thankfulness to Him that He condescended to die the death of the cross. I wish it were possible for us now to stand at the foot of the cross with Mary, and John, and the other disciples, and to hear the ribaldry and scorn for a moment, and then to look up, and see that sorrowful face, and that tortured body, and to read, in Hebrew, and Greek, and Latin, "Jesus of Nazareth, the King of the Jews." It was a very remarkable thing that Pilate should have written, as Matthew and Luke say that he did, "This is the King of the Jews," and we do not at all wonder that the chief priests said to Pilate, "Write not, the King of

This sermon was taken from *The Metropolitan Tabernacle Pulpit* and was preached on Sunday evening, December 6, 1874.

the Jews; but that He said, I am King of the Jews." But Pilate answered, "What I have written, I have written."

Divine providence always has its way. It matters not who may be the persons concerned, God knows how to work His own will with them. It was His purpose that His Son should not die upon the cross without a public proclamation of His innocence, and an official recognition that He was what He had said He was, namely, the King of the Jews. Who was to put up such a notice over His head as He hung there? Peter might have been bold enough to attempt to do it; but he would certainly not have succeeded, for the Roman legionaries jealously guarded every place of execution. Even John, daring as he might have been in such a crisis, could not have achieved the task. It was best that it should be done by authority, done by the Roman governor, done with an official pen, and so secured that no envious chief priest dared to pluck it down, and no hand of a scoffer could be uplifted to blot out its testimony. It was privileged writing because it was written by the pen of a Roman official, and there it must stay, under the authority of the Roman law, as long as the body of Jesus hung upon the cross. See what God can do. He can make the vacillating Pilate to become stubborn, and He can make him resolve to do what one would have thought would have been the last thing he would have done. Though his motive probably was to ridicule the Savior, yet the thing was done as God would have it, and Jesus on the cross hung there proclaimed by Roman authority as "the King of the Jews."

It may appear to you, at first sight, that there is not much importance in this fact, but I think I shall be able to show you that there is if you will sit down now, at the foot of the cross, and look up to your crucified Lord, and read this writing again. I shall ask you to read it in two lights; first, *in reference to man*; and, secondly, *in reference to Jesus Christ Himself.*

In Reference to Man

This is *a picture of how the world rejects the Savior*. The Savior had truly come into the world. That He might be known to be a Savior, He had taken the name of Jesus, that is, Savior. That He might be known as one who was very humble and lowly, He had condescended to dwell among men of the very humblest kind, and, therefore, He had chosen to dwell at Nazareth, and to be called the Nazarene. Thus He was known as Jesus, the Savior, and as Jesus of Nazareth, an approachable and lowly Savior. Jesus had come into the world to save men, and He had commenced His mission by saving many from diseases which had been regarded as incurable. He had opened blind eyes, unstopped deaf ears, given speech to the dumb, cleansing to lepers, and He had even raised the dead to life. There were many also whom He had healed of spiritual infirmities, for He had given faith to the faithless, and holiness and excellence of character to those who, until then, had lived in sin.

He was indeed Jesus the Savior, but how did men receive Him? Did they come and fall at His feet, and kiss the very dust He trod upon? One might not have been surprised if they had done so, but they did not. Did they gather around Him with joyful clamor, all sick ones eager to touch the hem of His garment that they might be made whole? There were a few who did so, "a remnant according to the election of grace" who received Him, and to them "he gave power to become the sons of God, even to them that believed on his name." But it was not so with the mass of mankind; discerning in Him something strange and singular, seeing in Him no enmity, no sinful anger, no pride, no bitterness, seeing in Him only superlative love, yet they must needs treat Him most foully, for His life was spent in poverty and reproach, and at last He was condemned to die on the accursed tree. The world hung Him up upon the felon's gibbet, and in doing so, men said, "This is the Savior, the Nazarene, and this is how we treat Him. We do not want to be saved from sin, for we love it. We do not want to be saved from rebellion, and to be brought into peace with God through Jesus Christ, so this is what we do with God's ambassador. This is how we serve Him who comes with words of reconciliation and grace upon His lips; we hang Him up to die, for we do not want Him." This is only a specimen of what all sinful hearts do; until they are changed by grace, they will not have the Savior to rule over them.

"Oh!" says someone, "you bring too harsh a charge against me!" Is it so? Have you received Jesus? Do you believe in Him? Has He become your Savior? If not, why not? Can you give any justifiable reason for your unbelief and rejection of Him? It seems to me, and I leave your conscience to decide whether it is so, that, by remaining in unbelief, you do practically say, "I prefer to be damned forever rather than believe in Jesus Christ." At any rate, that is your choice at this present moment; and if a man will show his objection to Christ to so great an extent that he would himself be cast into hell sooner than let Jesus save him, you may depend upon it that there dwells in his heart sufficient enmity to Christ to hang Him up again upon the gibbet if He were here once more. Christ would be hanged tomorrow if He came here among unregenerate hearts; aye, by the very people that hang their ivory crosses about their necks, and put them on their prayer books, and fix them on their walls. They would cry as their predecessors did of old, "Away with him, away with him, crucify him." To this day, when substitution is preached, and the blood of atonement, and salvation by simple faith in Jesus, and not by sacraments and priests and good works, men foam at the mouth with rage, for they still hate the Christ, the only

Savior of the sons of men.

Next, I see here that *man slays the incarnate God*: "Jesus of Nazareth the King of the Jews." Whether Pilate intended to indicate that He was the Messiah, at any rate the Jews saw that this would be the meaning attached to his inscription over Christ's head; it would be said that their Messiah was crucified, consequently they desired that the writing might be altered, but Pilate would not alter it. Now, the Messiah of the Jews was none other than God in human flesh. Did not Isaiah speak of Him as Immanuel, God with us? He was that promised seed of the woman who was to bruise the old serpent's head. This was He of whom David said, "The Lord said unto my lord, Sit thou at my right hand, until I make thine enemies thy footstool." He was David's Son, yet He was also David's Lord, and there He is: He has come among men, and as God He came to tabernacle in human flesh, and dwell among men. It is a wonderful story that tells us how He was found as a babe in Bethlehem's manger, where the shepherds came to adore Him, and how He grew up among men as a man like other men, working at the carpenter's bench in the shop of His reputed father, yet all the while He was God veiled beneath the humble form of the son of Mary. Even when the time came for His manifestation to Israel, He was still veiled, though His Godhead every now and then flashed through the veil of His humanity. He bade the sea be still when its wild uproar threatened to engulf the vessel in which He and His disciples were. He worked such wonders that it was clear that all things obeyed Him. The fish came in swarms from the deep to the net which He had bidden His disciples cast into the sea, and the loaves and fishes were multiplied in His hands and theirs, through His miraculous power. Men could not help seeing that He was more than man, and that He was indeed the Son of God, as He claimed to be.

Yet the husbandmen, to whom He was sent by His Father, to ask for the rent of the vineyard that had been let to them, said, "This is the heir; come, let us kill him, and let us seize on his inheritance." In other words, they said, "This is the God-man; let us do with Him what we would do with God if we could"; so they hanged Him up like a felon, and put a label above His head, as much as to say to God Himself, "This is what we have done to One who was more like You than any man we have ever heard of before, and One who says that He and You are one." O sirs, this wicked world never went so far in wickedness as it displayed on that occasion. The essence of every sin is enmity against God; and when any sin is analyzed, it is always found that its essence is this, "No God." Sin is a stab at the heart of God. Every time we sin, we practically say, "We do not want God's government; we do not want God's laws; we do not want God." I once heard an eloquent divine, who had been accusing men of great sin, finish his indictment by using this remarkable expression, "this deicidal world." There he reached the climax of truth, for this is a deicidal world. It cannot actually put God to death, but it would do so if it could; and in putting Christ to death it showed the enmity toward God that was really in its heart. The world would not put its own god to death, the god that men imagine, the god that their own intellects fabricate, the god like themselves, of whom I spoke this morning; but as for the God of the Bible, there are millions of men who would be glad to put that God out of His own universe if they could; yet He is Jehovah, the one living and true God.

Thirdly, I see here that *man's chief objection to Christ is His authority*; for the pith of that inscription was, "Jesus the *King*." Pilate did not write, "This is Jesus the Teacher," or many might have said, "Let him teach what He pleases, it is no concern of ours. We do not care what the seers see, or what they say." Pilate did not put up, "This is Jesus the Priest." Man would be quite content to let Him be the great High Priest if they also might be priests. But Pilate wrote, "This is Jesus the King," and that is the target at which they shoot all their arrows.

You remember that the writer of Psalm 2 says, "The kings of the earth set themselves, and the rulers take counsel together, against the Lord, and against his Anointed, saying, Let us break their bands asunder, and cast away their cords from us." The resolve of human nature until it is renewed is always this, "We will not have this Man to reign over us." Men might be willing for Christ to save them, but not for Him to reign over them. Such laws as these—"Thou shalt love thy neighbor as thyself," "Thou shalt forgive till seventy times seven," the law of love, the law of gentleness, the law of kindness, man says that he admires them, but when these laws come home to him, and lay hold of the reins of his ambition, cramp his covetousness, and condemn his self-righteousness, straightway he is offended; and when Christ says, "Heaven and earth shall pass away, but my words shall not pass away"; when He begins to teach the necessity of absolute purity, and to say that even a lascivious glance of the eye is a sin, then men reply, "His rule will never do for us," and they hang Him up to die because they will not submit to His authority.

Once more, we learn from this narrative that *man ridicules Christ's kingdom*. Pilate did not hate Christ; he probably did not think enough of Him to expend any of his hatred upon Him. I have no doubt that he thought that Jesus was a poor enthusiast, who had been living alone so long that He had addled His brains. He was well meaning, and perhaps clever; but, at the same time, not the sort of man for a Roman governor to dispute with. He was very sorry to have to put Him to death, for there were so many good points about the poor creature that he did not wish to let His enemies destroy Him. When the question of Christ's kingdom came up, I can imagine how scoffingly Pilate asked Him, "Art thou the King of the Jews?" How contemptuously he must have looked down upon such a poor emaciated creature, who seemed to be despised by everybody, as Christ said, "My kingdom is not of this world"; and Pilate asked, "Art thou a king then?" half laughing as he spoke. He must have felt as if he could fairly laugh Him to scorn, and I have no doubt that it was in that spirit that he wrote, "This is Jesus the King of the Jews," doing it in a vein of grim sardonic humor, first, toward the Jews, and secondly, toward Christ Himself, as much as to say, "This is the great King that the Jews have been looking for. They are going to fight Caesar, and get free, and this is the ringleader who is to help them to defeat all the legions of haughty Rome."

Amongst the ungodly, at the present day, the idea of a spiritual kingdom is quite beyond their comprehension; they cannot make out what it is. The relation between church and state will not be settled by the statesmen of any political party. There is a very singular relation between the two, though they are as dissimilar as materialism is from spirit. The realms of the two often overlap one another; you cannot draw a line, and say, "So far is the state, and so far is the church." The fact is, the true church of God is never subordinate to the state; it moves in another sphere altogether, and rules after another fashion. A spiritual kingdom, according to some people, means certain laws and regulations that are drawn up by the bishops and synods and councils, but that kind of kingdom is no more spiritual than an act passed by the House of Commons and the House of Lords. It is only another kingdom of the flesh, an ecclesiastical state of a similar kind to the secular state.

But as for the spiritual kingdom of Jesus Christ, it is not a thing that you can see with your eyes or understand after the manner of men. "Ye must be born again" in order to get into it, or even to see it. It is too ethereal to be checked by human legislation. It is a mighty power which Christ has set up in this world, a power mightier than all secular states combined, a kingdom like the stone cut out of the mountain without hands, which will break in pieces every other power, and fill the whole earth in God's appointed time. Oh, that we saw its power more manifest, nowadays, in the hearts of men, the power of that kingdom of which Christ is the King, and this blessed Book is the law, and the Holy Spirit is the great executive, and each of us is a servant in the courts of the great King living and acting according to His will.

"Oh!" you say, "that is ridiculous." Yes, I thought you would say that; that is what the world always says of the kingdom of Christ, that it is ridiculous. They can understand a kingdom in which there is a head like the pope, and in which there are cardinals, bishops, and priests; they can understand the archbishop of Canterbury, and the archbishop of York, and all that appertains to Episcopalianism; but to know that we are one with Christ, that He has made us kings and priests to God and His Father, that His saints are to reign with Him forever, and that the weapons of our warfare, though not carnal, are "mighty through God to the pulling down of strongholds"— they do not understand it, nor do they want to understand it. This is why they still hang up Christ the King and say, "If this is His kingdom, we do not want to belong to it, and we do not believe in it. Away with it; it is but worthy of our consideration; it is only a few low-minded fellows who will ever be the subjects of such a kingdom as that." This is "as it was in the beginning," and "is now," but not as it "ever shall be, world without end," for the King is coming, a second time, in all the splendor of His glory, and He will let the world know that, although His kingdom is not like others, and is not to be kept up by gold, and pomp, and rank, and dignity, and physical force, yet it is a kingdom which shall last when earthly princes and thrones shall all have passed away, and everyone who belongs to that kingdom shall possess a crown and a glory before which all the pomp of this world shall pale forever.

In Reference to Christ

What did that inscription over His head mean? It meant, first, that *Christ's honor was clear*. Look at the inscription over the head of that thief who is hanging on the next cross. "Put to death for robbery in the mountains, where he was taken red-handed, having stabbed one of the guards who attempted to arrest him." You quite understand that inscription, and you pass on to Jesus, and you want to know about the crime of which He has been guilty; you will be quite sure that they will put over His head an account of the worst thing He has ever done. There are the chief priests and scribes, and a multitude of the Jews watching to see what is written, and there is Pilate waiting to excuse his own conscience. If he can write anything that will exonerate him from the guilt of putting Christ to death, he will be sure to write it; so he takes his pen in his hand, and he writes, "This is Jesus of Nazareth, the King of the Jews." "Well," you say, "is that all that can be brought against Him, that He is Jesus of Nazareth, the King of the Jews?"

Yes, that is His only offense; they cannot sum up His guilt in any other words. His crime is that He is what He is, that He was a Savior, that He dwelt at Nazareth, and that He was the King of the Jews. Now, no exoneration of His character could be better than that of this official accusation against Him; and if this accusation brings nothing against Him, think how much may be said in His favor by His friends. When a man is brought before the judge, his accuser is quite sure to say all he can against him, and when Christ was about to be put to death, those who were responsible for that colossal crime had to make out as grave a charge against Him as they could. But this was all they could do; they could not bring anything else against Him except that He was Jesus of Nazareth, the King of the Jews. See, then, how absolutely without blemish and without spot was the Lamb of our Passover. See how He "knew no sin," though He was made a sin offering for us, "that we might be made the righteousness of God in him." Exult, Christians, in this public and official testimony to the spotless purity of His whole life and character.

Next, as far as Christ is concerned, we may view this inscription as *the explanation of His death* as well as the clearing of His character. Keep that superscription clearly in our mind's eye, "Jesus of Nazareth the King of the Jews." That is the reason why He died. Jesus died, first, because He was Jesus, because He was the Savior. That is the meaning of it; not that He might be made an example merely, not that He might bear witness to the truth only; but that cruel death means atonement, and salvation by atonement. Let us all look up to Him upon the cross. If we have done so before, let us look up to Him again, and say, "Yes, blessed Lord, we see that You did die, and that You did die to save us; and we magnify You because this was the cause of Your death, that You were the Savior." The whole title that Pilate wrote signified that Christ was the Messiah, and He died because He was the Messiah. "Messiah shall be cut off, but not for himself." This was the wonderful language of the prophet Daniel, "cut off, but not for himself"; cut off because He was the Sent One of God, the Anointed of the Most High. The prophet had also recorded the words of Jehovah, "Awake, O sword, against my shepherd, and against the man that is my fellow, saith the Lord of hosts." There, beloved, you have the whole reason for Christ's death condensed into a sentence. Jesus dies because He is the Savior, the anointed and prophesied Messiah, sent of God to be the King of the Jews, and of the Gentiles, too.

But, thirdly, as far as Christ was concerned, this inscription over His head was *a claim which was there and then announced.* He is hanging on the cross, and there is no trumpeter to make a proclamation of His kingship, but He does not need any such herald, for the same soldiers who fasten His hands to the wood fasten up an inscription which is the best proclamation possible, for it is in three different languages that all mankind may read it, "This is Jesus, the King of the Jews." He claims to be King, so stand at the foot of the cross, I pray you, and admit His claim. If you would have Jesus to be your Savior, you must have Him as your King; you must submit to His government, for He claims the right to rule over all who acknowledge Him to be Jesus; yes, more than that, He claims to rule all mankind, for all power is given to Him in heaven and in earth, and we are bidden to proclaim His kingdom throughout the whole world, and to, say to all men, "Jesus of Nazareth is your King, bow down before Him. Kings, bow before Him, for He is King of Kings; lords and nobles, bow before Him, for He is Lord of Lords; and all you sons and daughters of men, bow at His feet, for He must reign and even if you are His enemies, He must reign over you in spite of all your enmity and opposition, you must be brought to lie at His feet. The claims of Christ, therefore, were published even from the tree on which He died; so do not resist them, but willingly yield yourselves up to Jesus now and let Him be King to you henceforth and forever.

And, then, not only was a claim of His sovereignty made by the affixing of this title, but *His reign was there and then proclaimed*. In an earthly monarchy, as soon as one king is gone, it is usual to proclaim his successor and by that accusation written up over the head of Christ a proclamation was made throughout all the earth that Jesus had assumed the throne and He has never ceased to reign. He went back to His Father, and returned again to the earth, and dwelt here for forty days, and then His feet left mount Olivet, and He ascended to His throne, and there He sits "expecting till his enemies be made his footstool." His kingdom is established; do you all belong to it? It is a kingdom that, in a certain sense, was recognized on the cross by Pilate's proclamation, though it had existed long before, for His kingdom is an everlasting kingdom. Do you belong to it, or are you outside of it, opposed to it, or indifferent to it? Remember that He that is not with Christ is against Him. Those who are not on His side He reckons to be on the other side. Are you, my brother or sister, in the kingdom of the Lord Jesus Christ? If so, I know that you look with delight upon that inscription, and as you trust to the blood of Christ to cleanse you, you cast your eye up to that dear head that was crowned with thorns, and rejoice to think that Jesus of Nazareth, the King of the Jews, is also your King and Lord and Savior.

I want to make just this other remark about this inscription. Inasmuch as Pilate would not alter it, it seems to me that *God set forth to mankind that He would never have it altered*. Pilate could have sent for that inscription, and, with a few strokes of his pen, could have inserted the words that the chief priests wanted, "*He said*, I am King of the Jews." But Pilate would not do it, and the high priest could not do it, and the Devil could not do it, and all the devils in hell, and all the wicked men upon earth, with all their rages, cannot do it now. God has said it as well as Pilate, "What I have written I have written." "Yet have I set my king upon my holy hill of Zion." He must reign, and no power can ever take away His kingdom from Him! His church still prays, "Thy kingdom come," and that kingdom is yet to come in all its fullness when the whole of Israel shall be gathered together, and shall accept Him as their Lord and King. Yes, more than that, for "he shall have dominion also from sea to sea, and from the river unto the ends of the earth. They that dwell in the wilderness shall before him; and his enemies shall lick the dust . . . Yea, all kings shall fall down before him: all nations shall serve him."

Dearly beloved friends, this is the conclusion of the whole matter, *let us cheerfully accept Him as our King.* Have we done so? Then, let us try to push His conquests on yet further, and seek to extend the boundaries of His kingdom. Are you doing this? Then, do it yet more earnestly; and do it with the right instrument, for the great weapon of conquest is the Cross. It was on the cross that the proclamation was first lifted up, and it is by the Cross that it must be carried to the ends of the earth—not by human learning or eloquence, not by bribery, or the help of the state, and I know not what besides, but by the setting forth of Christ evidently crucified among the sons of men. The Cross is its own battle-ax, and weapon of war. "In this sign shalt thou conquer." Let the whole church preach Christ more, and live Christ more, and then the proclamation of His kingdom, which was first fastened up on that cross, shall be emblazoned throughout the whole world, and the power of His kingdom shall be felt to the very ends of the earth.

I looked into the darkness, and I thought I saw a cross before me, and I saw Him who did once hang upon it, but, as I looked at it, that cross seemed to grow. It seemed to become a tree, and I saw it strike its roots down deep, until the lowest depths of human misery had been touched and blessed by them. Then I saw that tree tower on high, piercing the clouds, passing through the very firmament up above the stars, lifting believers up upon it, and bearing them to the very throne of God by its majestic power. Then I saw that tree stretch forth its mighty branches on every side. Their shadow fell across this highly favored land of ours, and also fell across the lands on the other side of the sea. As I watched, the blessed branches stretched out to Europe, to Asia, to Africa, to America, and to Australia also. I watched it grow until it became so vast a tree that its shadow seemed to cover the whole earth, and I blessed and adored the God of heaven that He had instituted so mighty a power for the blessing of the sons of men. O Jesus, once crucified but now exalted, so let it be; and let us be Your humble instruments in promoting the extension of Your blessed reign; and we will ever adore You, as we do now, not only as "Jesus of Nazareth, the King of the Jews," but as the blessed and only Potentate, the King of Kings, and Lord of Lords; to whom be honor and power everlasting. Amen.

10

On the Cross After Death

The Jews therefore, because it was the preparation, that the bodies should not remain upon the cross on the Sabbath day (for that Sabbath day was an high day,) besought Pilate that their legs might be broken, and that they might be taken away. Then came the soldiers, and brake the legs of the first, and of the other which was crucified with him. But when they came to Jesus, and saw that he was dead already, they brake not his legs: but one of the soldiers with a spear pierced his side, and forthwith came there out blood and water. And he that saw it bare record, and his record is true: and he knoweth that he saith true, that ye might believe. For these things were done, that the scripture should be fulfilled, A bone of him shall not be broken. And again another scripture saith, They shall look on him whom they pierced (John 19:31–37).

Criminals who were crucified by the Romans were allowed to rot upon the crosses. That cruel nation can hardly be so severely condemned as our own people, who up to a late period allowed the bodies of those condemned to die to hang in chains upon gibbets in conspicuous places. The horrible practice is now abandoned, but it was retained to a time almost, if not quite, within living memory. I wonder whether any aged person here remembers such a horrible spectacle. Among the Romans it was usual, for there are classical allusions to this horror, showing that the bodies of persons crucified were usually left to be devoured by ravenous birds. Probably out of deference to the customs of the Jews, the authorities in Palestine would sooner or later allow of the interment of the crucified; but they would by no means hasten it, since they would not feel such a disgust at the sight as an Israelite would. The Mosaic law, which you will find in the book of

This sermon was taken from *The Metropolitan Tabernacle Pulpit* and was preached on Sunday morning, April 3, 1887.

Deuteronomy runs as follows—"If thou hang him on a tree, his body shall not remain all night upon the tree, but thou shalt in any wise bury him that day" (Deut. 21:22–23). This alone would lead the Jews to desire the burial of the executed but there was a further reason. Lest the land should be defiled upon the holy Sabbath of the Passover, the chief priests were importunate that the bodies of the crucified should be buried, and therefore that their deaths should be hastened by the breaking of their legs. Their consciences were not wounded by the murder of Jesus, but they were greatly moved by the fear of ceremonial pollution. Religious scruples may live in a dead conscience. Alas! this is not the only proof of that fact: we could find many in our own day.

The Jews hurried to Pilate, and sought as a boon the merciless act of having the legs of the crucified dashed to pieces with an iron bar. That act was sometimes performed upon the condemned as an additional punishment; but in this instance it was meant to be a finishing stroke, hastening death by the terrible pain which it would cause, and the shock to the system which it would occasion. Ferocious hate of our Lord made His enemies forgetful of everything like humanity: doubtless the more of pain and shame which they could cause to Him the better would they be pleased. Not, however, out of cruelty, but out of regard to the ceremonials of their religion, they "besought Pilate that their legs might be broken, and that they might be taken away." I have already told you that this breaking of the bones of the crucified was a Roman custom; and of this we have evidence, since there is a Latin word, *crucifragium*, to express this barbarous act. Pilate had no hesitation in granting the desire of the Jews: what would he care about the dead body, since he had already delivered up the living man?

Soldiers go at once to perform the hideous operation, and they commence with the two malefactors. It is a striking fact that the penitent thief, although he was to be in paradise with his Lord that day, was not, therefore, delivered from the excruciating agony occasioned by the breaking of his legs. We are saved from eternal misery, not from temporary pain. Our Savior, by our salvation, gives no pledge to us that we shall be screened from suffering in this life. It is true, as the proverb has it, "All things come alike to all: there is one event to the righteous, and to the wicked; to the clean, and to the unclean." Accidents and diseases afflict the godly as well as the ungodly. Penitent or impenitent, we share the common lot of men, and are born to troubles as the sparks fly upward. You must not expect because you are pardoned, even if you have the assurance of it from Christ's own lips, that, therefore, you shall escape tribulation; no, but from His precious mouth you have the forewarning assurance that trial shall befall you; for Jesus said, "These things I have spoken unto you, that in me ye might have peace. In the world ye shall have tribulation." Suffering is not averted, but it is turned into a blessing. The penitent thief entered into paradise that very day, but it was not without suffering say; rather, that the terrible stroke was the actual means of the prompt fulfillment of his Lord's promise to him. By that blow he died that day; else might he have lingered long. How much we may any of us receive by the way of suffering it were hard to guess: perhaps, the promise that we shall be with our Lord in paradise will be fulfilled that way.

At this point it seemed more than probable that our blessed Lord must undergo the breaking of His bones; but "he was dead already." It had pleased Him, in the infinite willingness with which He went to His sacrifice, to yield up His life, and His spirit had therefore departed. Yet one might have feared that the coarse soldiers would have performed their orders to the letter. See, they do not so! Had they conceived a dread of one around whom such prodigies had gathered? Were they, like their centurion, impressed with awe of this remarkable personage? At any rate, perceiving that He was dead already, they did not use their hammer. Happy are we to see them cease from such loathsome brutality. But we may not be too glad, for another outrage will take its place: to make sure that He was dead, one of the four soldiers with a spear pierced His side, probably thrusting his lance quite through the heart. Here we see how our gracious God ordained in His providence that there should be sure evidence that Jesus was dead, and that therefore the sacrifice was slain. Paul declares this to be the Gospel, that the Lord Jesus died according to the Scriptures. Strange to say, there have been heretics who have ventured to assert that Jesus did not actually die. They stand refuted by this spear-thrust. If our Lord did not die, then no sacrifice has been presented, the Resurrection is not a fact, and there is no foundation of hope for men. Our Lord assuredly died, and was buried: the Roman soldiers were keen judges in such matters, and they saw that "he was dead already," and, moreover, their spears were not used in vain when they meant to make death a certainty.

When the side of Christ was pierced, there flowed thereout blood and water, upon which a great deal has been said by those who think it proper to dilate upon such tender themes. It was supposed by some that by death the blood was divided, the clots parting from the water in which they float, and that in a perfectly natural way. But it is not true that blood could flow from a dead body if it were pierced. Only under certain very special conditions would blood gush forth. The flowing of this blood from the side of our Lord cannot be considered as a common occurrence: it was a fact entirely by itself. We cannot argue from any known fact in this case, for we are here in a new region. Granted, that blood would not flow from an ordinary dead body; yet remember, that our Lord's body was unique, since it saw no corruption. Whatever change might come over a body liable to decay, we may not ascribe any such change to His frame; and therefore there is no arguing from facts about common bodies so as to conclude therefrom anything concerning our blessed Lord's body. Whether, in His case, blood and water flowed naturally from His holy and incorruptible body, or whether it was a miracle, it was evidently a most notable and remarkable thing, and John, as an eyewitness, was evidently astonished at it, and so astonished at it that he recorded a solemn affirmation, in order that we might not doubt his testimony. He was certain of what he saw, and he took care to report it with a special note, in order that we might believe; as if he felt that if this fact was truly believed, there was a certain convincing power which would induce many to believe on our Lord Jesus as the appointed Savior. I could enter into many details, but I prefer to cast a veil over this tender mystery. It is scarcely reverent to be discoursing of anatomy when the body of our adorable Lord is before us. Let us close our eyes in worship rather than open them with irreverent curiosity.

The great task before me this morning is to draw truth out of this well of wonders. I shall ask you to look at the events before us in three lights: first, let us see here *the fulfillment of Scripture*; secondly, *the identification of our Lord as the Messiah*; and thirdly, *the instruction which He intends*.

The Fulfillment of Scripture

Two things are predicted: not a bone of Him must be broken, and He must be pierced. These were the Scriptures which now remained to be accomplished. Last Lord's Day morning we were all of us delighted as we saw the fulfillment of Scripture in the capture of our Lord, and His refusal to deliver Himself from His enemies. The theme of the fulfillment of Scripture is worth pursuing yet further in an age when Holy Scripture is treated with so much slight, and is spoken of as having no inspiration in it, or, at least, no divine authority by which its infallibility is secured. You and I favor no such error; on the contrary, we conceive it to be to the last degree mischievous. "If the foundations be removed, what can the righteous do?" We are pleased to notice how the Lord Jesus Christ and those who wrote concerning Him treated the Holy Scriptures with an intensely reverent regard. The prophecies that went before of Christ must be fulfilled, and holy souls found great delight in dwelling upon the fact that they were so.

I want you to notice concerning this case, that *it was singularly complicated*. It was negative and positive: the Savior's bones must not be broken, and He must be pierced. In the type of the Passover lamb it was expressly enacted that not a bone of it should be broken; therefore not a bone of Jesus must be broken. At the same time, according to Zechariah 12:10, the Lord must be pierced. He must not only be pierced with the nails, and so fulfill the prophecy, "They pierced my hands and my feet"; but He must be conspicuously pierced, so that He can be emphatically regarded as a pierced one. How were these prophecies, and a multitude more, to be accomplished? Only God Himself could have brought to pass the fulfillment of prophecies which were of all kinds, and appeared to be confused, and even in contradiction to each other. It would be an impossible task for the human intellect to construct so many prophecies, and types, and foreshadowings, and then to imagine a person in whom they should all be embodied. But what would be impossible to men has been literally carried out in the case of our Lord. There are prophecies about Him and about everything connected with Him, from His hair to His garments, from His birth to His tomb, and yet they have all been carried out to the letter. That which lies immediately before us was a complicated case, for if reverence to the Savior would spare His bones, would it not also spare His flesh? If a coarse brutality pierced His side, why did it not break His legs? How can men be kept from one act of violence, and that an act authorized by authority, and yet how shall they perpetrate another violence which had not been suggested to them? But, let the case be as complicated as it was possible for it to have been, infinite wisdom knew how to work it out in all points; and it did so. The Christ is the exact substance of the foreshadowings of the Messianic prophecies.

Next, we may say of the fulfillment of these two prophecies, that it *was specially improbable*. It did not seem at all likely that when the order was given to break the legs of the crucified, Roman soldiers would abstain from the deed. How could the body of Christ be preserved after such an order had been issued? Those four soldiers are evidently determined to carry out the governor's orders; they have commenced their dreadful task, and they have broken the legs of two of the executed three. The crosses were arranged so that Jesus was hanging in the midst: He is the second of the three. We naturally suppose that they would proceed in order from the first cross to the second; but they seem to pass by the second cross, and proceed from the first to the third. What was the reason of this singular procedure? The supposition is, and I think a very likely one, that the center cross stood somewhat back, and that thus the two thieves formed a sort of first rank. Jesus would thus be all the more emphatically "in the midst." If He was placed a little back, it would certainly have been easier for the penitent thief to have read the inscription over His head, and to have looked to our Lord, and held conversation with Him. Had they been placed exactly in a line this might not have been so natural; but the suggested position seems to suit the circumstances. If it were so, I can understand how the soldiers would be taking the crosses in order when they performed their horrible office upon the two malefactors, and came last to Jesus, who was in the midst. In any case, such was the order which they followed. The marvel is that they did not in due course proceed to deal the horrible blow in the case of our Lord. Roman soldiers are apt to fulfill their commissions very literally, and they are not often moved with much desire to avoid barbarities. Can you see them intent upon their errand? Will they not even now mangle that sacred body? Commend me for roughness to the ordinary Roman soldier: he was so used to deeds of slaughter, so accustomed to an empire which had been established with blood and iron, that the idea of pity never crossed his soul, except to be scouted as a womanly feeling unworthy of a brave man. Yet behold and wonder! The order is given to break their legs: two out of the three have suffered, and yet no soldier may crush a bone of that sacred body. They see that He is dead already, and they break not His legs.

As yet you have only seen one of the prophecies fulfilled. He must be pierced as well. And what was that which came into that Roman soldier's mind when, in a hasty moment, he resolved to make sure that the apparent death of Jesus was a real one? Why did he open that sacred side with his lance? He knew nothing of the prophecy; he had no dreams of Eve being taken from the side of the man, and the church from the side of Jesus. He had never heard that ancient notion of the side of Jesus being like the door of the ark, through which an entrance to safety is opened. Why, then, does he fulfill the prediction of the prophet? There was no accident or chance here. Where are there such things? The hand of the Lord is here, and we desire to praise and bless that omniscient and omnipotent Providence which thus fulfilled the word of revelation. God has respect to His own word, and while He takes care that no bone of His Son shall be broken, He also secures that no text of Holy Scripture shall be broken. That our Lord's bones should remain unbroken, and yet that He should be pierced, seemed a very unlikely thing; but it was carried out. When next you meet with an unlikely promise, believe it firmly. When next you see things working contrary to the truth of God, believe God, and believe nothing else. Let God be true and every man a liar. Though men and devils should give God the lie, hold you on to what God has spoken; for heaven and earth shall pass away, but not one jot or tittle of His word shall fall to the ground.

Note again, dear friends, concerning this fulfillment of Scripture, that *it was altogether indispensable.* If they had broken Christ's bones, then that word of John the Baptist, "Behold the Lamb of God," had seemed to have a slur cast upon it. Men would have objected, "But the bones of the Lamb of God were not broken." It was especially commanded twice over, not only in the first ordaining of the Passover in Egypt, but in the allowance of a second to those who were defiled at the time of the first Passover. In Numbers, as well as in Exodus, we read that not a bone of the lamb must be broken. How, then, if our Lord's bones had been broken, could we have said, "Christ our Passover is sacrificed for us," when there would have been this fatal flaw? Jesus must remain intact upon the cross, and He must also be pierced; for else that famous passage in Zechariah, which is here alluded to, "They shall look on me whom they have pierced," could not have been true of Him. Both prophecies must be carried out, and they were so in a conspicuous manner.

But why need I say that this fulfillment was indispensable? Beloved, the keeping of every word of God is indispensable. It is indispensable to the truth of God that He should be true always: for if one word of His can fall to the ground, then all may fall, and His veracity is gone. If it can be demonstrated that one prophecy was a mistake, then all the rest may be mistakes. If one part of the Scripture is untrue, all may be untrue, and we have no sure ground to go upon; faith loves not slippery places; faith seeks the sure word of prophecy, and sets her foot firmly upon certainties. Unless all the Word of God is sure, and pure "as silver tried in a furnace of earth, purified seven times," then we have nothing to go upon, and are virtually left without a revelation from God. If I am to take the Bible and say, "Some of this is true, and some of it is questionable," I am no better off than if I had no Bible. A man who is at sea with a chart which is only accurate in certain places is not much better off than if he had no chart at all. I see not how it can ever be safe to be "converted and become as little children" if there is no infallible teacher for us to follow. Beloved, it is indispensable to the honor of God and to our confidence in His Word, that every line of Holy Scripture should be true. It was indispensable evidently in the case now before us, and this is only one instance of a rule which is without exception.

But now let me remind you that although the problem was complicated, and its working out was improbable, yet *it was fulfilled in the most natural manner*. Nothing can be less constrained than the action of the soldiers; they have broken the legs of two, but the other is dead, and they do not break His legs; yet, to make sure that they will be safe in omitting the blow, they pierce His side. There was no compulsion put upon them; they did this of their own proper thought. No angel came from heaven to stand with his broad wings in the front of the cross, so as to protect the Savior; no awful aegis of mystery was hung over the sacred body of the Lord so that intruders might be driven back with fear. No, the quaternion of soldiers did whatever they wished to do. They acted of their own free will, and yet at the same time they fulfilled the eternal counsel of God. Shall we never be able to drive into men's minds the truth that predestination and free agency are both facts? Men sin as freely as birds fly in the air, and they are altogether responsible for their sin; and yet everything is ordained and foreseen of God. The foreordination of God in no degree interferes with the responsibility of man. I have often been asked by persons to reconcile the two truths. My only reply is—They need no reconciliation, for they never fell out. Why should I try to reconcile two friends? Prove to me that the two truths do not agree. In that request I have set you a task as difficult as that which you propose to me. These two facts are parallel lines; I cannot make them unite but you cannot make them cross each other. Permit me also to add that I have long ago given up the idea of making all my beliefs into a system. I believe, but I cannot explain. I fall before the majesty of revelation, and adore the infinite Lord. I do not understand all that God reveals, but I believe it. How can I expect to understand all the mysteries of revelation, when even the arithmetic of Scripture surpasses my comprehension, since I am taught that in the Godhead the Three are One, while in the undivided One I see most manifestly Three? Need I measure the sea? Is it not enough that I am upborne by its waves? I thank God for waters deep enough for my faith to swim in: understanding would compel me to keep to the shallows, but faith takes me to the main ocean. I think it more to my soul's benefit to believe than to understand, for faith brings me nearer to God than reason ever did. The faith which is limited by our narrow faculties is a faith unworthy of a child of God; for as a child of God he should begin to deal with infinite sublimities, like those in which his great Father is at home. These are only to be grasped by faith. To return to my subject: albeit the matter must be as Scripture foreshadowed, yet no constraint nor inducement was put forth; but, as free agents, the soldiers performed the very things which were written in the Prophets concerning Christ.

Dear friends, suffer one more observation upon this fulfillment of Scripture: *it was marvelously complete*. Observe that in these transactions a seal was set upon that part of Scripture which has been most exposed to skeptical derision: for the seal was set first of all upon *the types*. Irreverent readers of Scripture have refused to accept the types: they say, "How do you know that the Passover was a type of Christ? In other cases, more serious persons object to detailed interpretations, and decline to see a meaning in the smaller particulars. Such persons would not attach spiritual importance to the law, "Not a bone of it shall be broken"; but would dismiss it as a petty regulation of an obsolete religious rite. But observe, beloved, the Holy Spirit does nothing of the kind; for He fixes upon a minor particular of the type, and declares that this must be fulfilled. Moreover, the providence of God intervenes, so that it shall be carried out. Wherefore, be not scared away from the study of the types by the ridicule of the worldly-wise. There is a general timidity coming over the minds of many about Holy Scripture, a timidity to which, thank God, I am an utter stranger. It would be a happy circumstance if the childlike reverence of the early fathers could be restored to the church, and the present irreverent criticism could be repented of and cast away. We may delight ourselves in the types as in a very paradise of revelation. Here we see our best Beloved's beauties mirrored in ten thousand delightful ways. There is a world of holy teaching in the books of the Old Testament, and in their types and symbols. To give up this patrimony of the saints, and to accept criticism instead of it, would be like selling one's birthright for a mess of pottage. I see in our Lord's unbroken bones a setting of the seal of God upon the types of Scripture.

Let us go further. I see, next, the seal of God set upon *unfulfilled prophecy*; for the passage in Zechariah is not yet completely fulfilled. It runs thus: "They shall look upon me whom they have pierced." Jehovah is the speaker, and He speaks of "the house of David and the inhabitants of Jerusalem." They are to look on Jehovah whom they have pierced, and to mourn for Him. Although this prophecy is not yet fulfilled on the largest scale, yet it is so far certified, for Jesus is pierced; the rest of it, therefore, stands good, and Israel shall one day mourn because of her insulted King. The prophecy was fulfilled in part when Peter stood up and preached to the Eleven, when a great company of the priests believed, and when multitudes of the seed of Abraham became preachers of Christ crucified. Still it awaits a larger fulfillment, and we may rest quite sure that the day shall come when all Israel shall be saved. As the piercing of their Lord is true, so shall the piercing of their hearts be true, and they shall mourn and inwardly bleed with bitter sorrow for Him whom they despised and abhorred. The point to mark here is, that a seal is set in this case to a prophecy which yet awaits its largest fulfillment; wherefore, we may regard this as a pattern, and may lay stress upon prophecy, and rejoice in it, and receive it without doubt, come what may.

I have said this much upon the fulfillment of the Word concerning our Lord; let us learn hence a lesson of reverence and confidence in reference to Holy Scripture.

The Identification of Our Lord as the Messiah

But now, secondly, and briefly, the identification of our Lord as the Messiah was greatly strengthened by that which befell His body after death. It was needful that He should conclusively be proved to be the Christ spoken of in the Old Testament. Certain marks and tokens are given, and those marks and tokens must be found in Him: they were so found.

The first mark was this: *God's Lamb must have a measure of preservation.* If Christ be what He professes to be, He is the Lamb of God. Now, God's lamb could only be dealt with in God's way. Yes, there is the lamb kill it, sprinkle its blood, roast it with fire, but break not its bones. It is God's lamb, and not yours, therefore hitherto shalt thou come, but no further. Not a bone of it shall be broken. Roast it, divide it among yourselves, and eat it, but break no bone of it. The Lord claims it as His own, and this is His reserve. So, in effect, the Lord says concerning the Lord Jesus: "There is my Son; bind Him, scourge Him, spit on Him, crucify Him; but He is the Lamb of my Passover, and you must not break a bone of Him." The Lord's right to Him is declared by the reservation which is made concerning His bones. Do you not see here how He is identified as being "the Lamb of God, which taketh away the sin of the world"? It is a mark of identity upon which faith fixes her eyes, and she studies that mark until she sees much more in it than we can this morning speak about, for we have other things to dwell upon.

The next mark of identity must be, that *Jehovah our Lord should be pierced by Israel.* So Zechariah said, and so must it be fulfilled. Not merely must His hands and feet be nailed, but most conspicuously must He be pierced. "They shall look upon me whom they have pierced, and they shall mourn for him." Pierced He must be. His wounds are the marks and tokens of His being the real Christ. When they shall see the sign of the Son of man in the last days, then shall all the tribes of the earth mourn; and is not that sign His appearing as a Lamb that has been slain? The wound in His side was a sure mark of His identity to His own disciples; for He said to Thomas, "Reach hither thy hand, and thrust it into my side: and be not faithless, but believing." It shall be the convincing token to all Israel: "They shall look upon me whom they have pierced, and they shall mourn for him, as one that mourneth for his only son." To us the opened way to His heart is in His flesh, the token that this is the incarnate God of love, whose heart can be reached by all who seek His grace.

But I have not finished this identification; for observe, that when that side was pierced, "forthwith came there out blood and water." You that have your Bibles will have opened them already at Zechariah 12. Will you kindly read on until you come to the first verse of the thirteenth chapter, which ought not to have been divided from the twelfth chapter? What do you find there? "In that day there shall be a fountain opened to the house of David and to the inhabitants of Jerusalem for sin and for uncleanness." They pierced Him, and in that day they began to mourn for Him; but more, in that day there was a fountain opened. And what was that fountain but this gush of water and of blood from the riven side of our redeeming Lord? The prophecies follow quickly upon one another; they relate to the same person, and to the same day; and we are pleased to see that the facts also follow quickly upon one another; for when the soldier with the spear pierced the side of Jesus, "*forthwith* came there out blood and water." Jehovah was pierced, and men repented, and beheld the cleansing fountain within a brief space. The men who saw the sacred fountain opened rejoiced to see in it the attestation of the finished sacrifice, and the token of its cleansing effect.

The identification is more complete if we add one more remark. Take all the types of the Old Testament together, and you will gather this, that the purification of sin was typically set forth by blood and water. Blood was conspicuous always, you have no remission of sin without it; but water was exceedingly prominent also. The priests before sacrificing must wash, and the victim itself must be washed with water. Impure things must be washed with running water. Behold how our Lord Jesus came by water and by blood; not by water only, but by water and blood. John who saw the marvelous stream never forgot the sight; for though he wrote his epistles, I suppose, far on in life, the recollection of that wondrous scene was fresh with him. Though I suppose he did not write his gospel until he was a very old man, yet when he came to this passage it impressed him as much as ever, and he uttered affirmations which he was not at all accustomed to use: "He that saw it bare record, and his record is true: and he knoweth that he saith true." In solemn form he thus, after a manner, gave his affidavit before God's people, that he did really behold this extraordinary sight. In Jesus we see one who has come to atone and to sanctify. He is that High Priest who cleanses the leprosy of sin by blood and water. This is one part of the sure identification of the great purifier of God's people, that He came both by water and by blood, and poured out both from His pierced side. I leave these identifications to you. They are striking to my own mind, but they are only part of the wonderful system of marks and tokens by which it is seen that God attests the man Christ Jesus as being in very deed the true Messiah.

The Instruction Intended for Us

The first instruction intended for us must be only hinted at, like all the rest. *See what Christ is to us.* He is the Paschal Lamb, not a bone of which was broken. You believe it. Come, then, and act upon your belief by feeding upon Christ; keep the feast in your own souls this day. That sprinkled blood of His has brought you safety: the destroying angel cannot touch you or your house. The Lamb Himself has become your food; feed on Him; remove your spiritual hunger by receiving Jesus into your heart. This is the food whereof if a man eat he shall live forever. Be filled with all the fullness of God, as you now receive the Lord Jesus as God and man. "Ye are complete in him." Ye are "perfect in Jesus Christ." Can you not say of Him: "He is all my salvation, and all my desire"? "Christ is all and in all." Do not merely learn this lesson as a doctrine, but enjoy it as a personal experience. Jesus our Passover is slain, let Him be eaten. Let us feast on Him, and then be ready to journey through the wilderness, in the strength of this divine meat, until we come to the promised rest.

What next do we learn from this lesson but this? See *man's treatment of Christ*. They have spit upon Him, they have cried, "Crucify him, crucify him," they have nailed Him to the cross, they have mocked His agonies, and He is dead; but man's malice is not glutted yet. The last act of man to Christ must be to pierce Him through. That cruel wound was the concentration of man's ill-treatment of Jesus. His experience at the hands of our race is summed up in the fact that they pierced Him to the heart. That is what men have done to Christ: they have so despised and rejected Him that He dies, pierced to the heart. Oh, the depravity of our nature! Some doubt whether it is total depravity. It deserves a worse adjective than that. There is no word in human language which can express the venom of the enmity of man to his God and Savior: he would wound Him mortally if he could. Do not expect that men will love either Christ or you, if you are like Him. Do not expect that Jesus will find room for Himself in the inn, much less that He will be set on the throne by guilty, unrenewed men. Oh, no! Even when He is dead they must insult His corpse with a spear thrust. One soldier did it, but he expressed the sentiment of the age. This is what the world of sinners did for Him who came into the world to save it.

Now, learn, in the next place, *what Jesus did for men*. Beloved, that was a sweet expression in our hymn just now—

> Even after death his heart
> For us its tribute poured.

In his life He had bled for us: drop by drop the bloody sweat had fallen to the ground. Then the cruel scourges drew from Him purple streams; but as a little store of lifeblood was left near His heart, He poured it all out before He went His way. It is a materialistic expression, but there is something more in it than mere sentiment—that there remains among the substance of this globe a sacred relic of the Lord Jesus in the form of that blood and water. As no atom of matter ever perishes, that matter remains on earth even now. His body has gone into glory, but the blood and water are left behind. I see much more in this fact than I will now attempt to tell. O world, the Christ has marked you with His blood and He means to have you! Blood and water from the heart of God's own Son have fallen down upon this dark and defiled planet, and thus Jesus has sealed it as His own, and as such it must be transformed into a new heaven and a new earth, wherein dwells righteousness. Our dear Lord, when He had given us all He had, and even resigned His life on our behalf, then parted with a priceless stream from the fountain of His heart: "forthwith came there out blood and water." Oh, the kindness of the heart of Christ, that did not only for a blow return a kiss, but for a spear thrust returned streams of life and healing!

But I must hurry on. I can see in this passage also *the safety of the saints*. It is marvelous how full of eyes the things of Jesus are; for His unbroken bones look backward to the Paschal lamb, but they also look forward throughout all the history of the church to that day when He shall gather all His saints in one body, and none shall be missing. Not a bone of His mystical body shall be broken. There is a text in the psalms which says of the righteous man—and all righteous men are conformed to the image of Christ—"He keepeth all his bones: not one of them is broken." I do rejoice in the safety of Christ's elect; He shall not permit a bone of His redeemed body to be broken.

> For all the chosen seed
> Shall meet around the throne,
> Shall bless the conduct of his grace,
> And make his glories known.

A perfect Christ there shall be in the day of His appearing, when all the members of His body shall be joined to their glorious Head, who shall be crowned forever. Not one living member of Christ shall be absent; "Not a bone of him shall be broken." There shall be no lame, maimed Christ, no half-wrought redemption; but the purpose that He came to accomplish shall be perfectly achieved to the glory of His name.

I have not quite done, for I must add another lesson. *We see here the salvation of sinners*. Jesus Christ's side is pierced to give to sinners the double cure of sin, the taking away of its guilt and power; but, better than this, sinners are to have their hearts broken by a sight of the Crucified. By this means also they are to obtain faith. "They shall look upon me whom they have pierced, and they shall mourn for him." Beloved, our Lord Jesus came not only to save sinners, but to seek them: His death not only saves those who have faith, but it creates faith in those who have it not. The Cross produces the faith and repentance which it demands. If you cannot come to Christ *with* faith and repentance, come to Christ for faith and repentance, for He can give them to you. He is pierced on purpose that you may be pricked to the heart. His blood, which freely flows, is shed for many for the remission of sins. What you have to do is just to look, and, as you look, those blessed feelings which are the marks of conversion and regeneration shall be wrought in you by a sight of Him. Oh, blessed lesson! Put it into practice this morning. Oh, that in this great house many may now have done with self and look to the crucified Savior, and find life eternal in Him! For this is the main end of John's writing this record, and this is the chief design of our preaching upon it: we long that you may believe. Come, guilty, come and trust the Son of God who died for you. Come, foul and polluted, come and wash in this sacred stream poured out for you. There is life in a look at the Crucified One. There is life at this moment for every one of you who will look to Him. God grant you may look and live, for Jesus Christ's sake! Amen.

11

The Three Hours' Darkness

Now from the sixth hour there was darkness over all the land unto the ninth hour (Matthew 27:45).

From nine until noon the usual degree of light was present; so that there was time enough for our Lord's adversaries to behold and insult His sufferings. There could be no mistake about the fact that He was really nailed to the cross for He was crucified in broad daylight. We are fully assured that it was Jesus of Nazareth, for both friends and foes were eyewitnesses of His agonies: for three long hours the Jews sat down and watched Him on the cross, making jests of His miseries. I feel thankful for those three hours of light for else the enemies of our faith would have questioned whether in very deed the blessed body of our Master was nailed to the tree, and would have started fancies as many as the bats and owls which haunt the darkness. Where would have been the witnesses of this solemn scene if the sun had been hidden from morn until night? As three hours of light gave opportunity for inspection and witness bearing, we see the wisdom which did not allow it to close too soon.

Never forget that this miracle of the closing of the eye of day at high noon was performed by our Lord in His weakness. He had walked the sea and raised the dead and healed the sick in the days of His strength; but now He has come to His lowest, the fever is on Him, He is faint and thirsty. He hangs on the borders of dissolution yet has He power to darken the sun at noon. He is still very God of very God:

> Behold, a purple torrent run
> Down from his hands and head,
> The crimson tide puts out the son;
> His groans awake the dead.

This sermon was taken from *The Metropolitan Tabernacle Pulpit* and was preached on Sunday morning, April 18, 1886.

If He can do this in His weakness, what is He not able to do in His strength? Fail not to remember that this power was displayed in a sphere in which He did not usually put forth His might. The sphere of Christ is that of goodness and benevolence, and consequently of light. When He enters the sphere of darkness making, and of working judgment, He engages in what He calls His strange work. Wonders of terror are His left-handed deeds. It is but now and then that He causes the sun to go down at noon, and darkens the earth in the clear day (Amos 8:9). If our Lord can make darkness at will as He dies, what glory may we not expect now that He lives to be the light of the city of God forever? The Lamb is the light; and what a light! The heavens bear the impress of His dying power, and lose their brightness; shall not the new heavens and the new earth attest the power of the risen Lord? The thick darkness around the dying Christ is the robe of the Omnipotent: He lives again, all power is in His hands, and all that power He will put forth to bless His chosen.

What a call must that midday midnight have been to the careless sons of men! They knew not that the Son of God was among them, nor that He was working out human redemption. The grandest hour in all history seemed likely to pass by unheeded, when, suddenly, night hastened from her chambers and usurped the day. Every one asked his fellow, "What means this darkness?" Business stood still: the plow stayed in midfurrow, and the ax paused uplifted. It was the middle of the day, when men are busiest; but they made a general pause. Not only on Calvary, but on every hill, and in every valley, the gloom settled down. There was a halt in the caravan of life. None could move unless they groped their way like the blind. The master of the house called for a light at noon, and his servant tremblingly obeyed the unusual summons. Other lights were twinkling, and Jerusalem was as a city by night, only men were not in their beds. How startled were mankind. Around the great deathbed an appropriate quiet was secured.

I doubt not that a shuddering awe came over the masses of the people, and the thoughtful foresaw terrible things. Those who had stood about the cross, and had dared to insult the majesty of Jesus, were paralyzed with fear. They ceased their ribaldry, and with it their cruel exultation. They were cowed though not convinced, even the basest of them; while the better sort "smote their breasts and returned." As many as could do so, no doubt, stumbled to their chambers, and endeavored to hide themselves, for fear of awful judgments which they feared were near. I do not wonder that there should be traditions of strange things that were said during the hush of that darkness. Those whispers of the past may or may not be true; they have been the subject of learned controversy, but the labor of the dispute was energy ill spent. Yet we could not have wondered if one did say as he is reported to have done, "God is suffering, or the world is perishing." Nor should I drive from my beliefs the poetic legend that an Egyptian pilot passing down the river heard among the reedy banks a voice out of the rustling rushes, whispering, "The great Pan is dead." Truly, the God of nature was expiring, and things less tender than the reeds by the river might well tremble at the sound thereof.

We are told that this darkness was over all the land; and Luke puts it, "over all the earth." That portion of our globe which was then veiled in natural night was not affected thereby, but to all men awake, and at their employment, it was the advertisement of a great and solemn event. It was strange beyond all experience, and all men marveled; for when the light should have been brightest, all things were obscured for the space of three hours.

There must be great teaching in this darkness; for when we come so near the Cross, which is the center of history, every event is full of meaning. Light will come out of this darkness. I love to feel the solemnity of the three hours of death-shade, and to sit down therein and meditate, with no companion but the august sufferer, around whom that darkness lowered. I am going to speak of it in four ways, as the Holy Spirit may help me. First, let us bow our spirits in the presence of *a miracle which amazes us*; secondly, let us regard this darkness as *a veil which conceals*; thirdly, as *a symbol which instructs*; and fourthly, as *a display of sympathy*.

A Miracle Which Amazes Us

It may seem a trite observation that this darkness was altogether out of the natural course of things. Since the world began was it not heard that at high noon there should be darkness over all the land. It was out of the order of nature altogether. Some deny miracles and if they also deny God, I will not at this time deal with them. But it is very strange that any one who believes in God should doubt the possibility of miracles. It seems to me that, granted the being of a God, miracle is to be expected as an occasional declaration of His independent and active will. He may make certain rules for His actions, and it may be His wisdom to keep to them; but surely He must reserve to Himself the liberty to depart from His own laws, or else He has in a measure laid aside His personal Godhead, deified law, and set it up above Himself. It would not increase our idea of the glory of His Godhead if we could be assured that He had made Himself subject to rule, and tied His own hands from ever acting except in a certain manner. From the self-existence and freedom of will which enter into our very conception of God, we are led to expect that sometimes He should not keep to the methods

which He follows as His general rule. This has led to the universal conviction that miracle is a proof of Godhead. The general works of creation and providence are to my mind the best proofs but the common
heart of our race, for some reason or other, looks to miracle as surer evidence; thus proving that miracle is expected of God. Although the
Lord makes it His order that there shall be day and night, He in this
case with abundant reason interposes three hours of night in the center
of a day. Behold the reason. The unusual in lower nature is made to
consort with the unusual in the dealings of nature's Lord. Certainly this
miracle was most congruous with that greater miracle which was hap-
pening in the death of Christ. Was not the Lord Himself departing from
all common ways? Was He not doing that which had never been done
from the beginning, and would never be done again? That man should
die is so common a thing as to be deemed inevitable. We are not startled now at the sound of a funeral knell: we have become familiar with
the grave. As the companions of our youth die at our side we are not
seized with amazement, for death is everywhere about us and within us.
But that the Son of God should die, this is beyond all expectation, and
not only above nature, but contrary thereto. He who is equal with God
deigns to hang upon the cross, and die. I know of nothing that seems
more out of rule and beyond expectation than this. The sun darkened at
noon is a fit accompaniment of the death of Jesus. Is it not so?

Further, this miracle was not only out of the order of nature, but it
was one which *would have been pronounced impossible*. It is not possible that there should be an eclipse of the sun at the time of the full
moon. The moon at the time when she is in her full is not in a position
in which she could possibly cast her shadow upon the earth. The
Passover was at the time of the full moon, and therefore it was not possible that the sun should then undergo an eclipse. This darkening of the
sun was not strictly an astronomical eclipse; the darkness was doubtless
produced in some other way: yet to those who were present it did seem
to be a total eclipse of the sun—a thing impossible. Ah, brothers! when
we come to deal with man and the fall and sin and God and Christ and
the atonement, we are at home with impossibilities. We have now
reached a region where prodigies and marvels and surprises are the
order of the day; sublimities become commonplaces when we come
within the circle of eternal love. Yes, more; we have now quitted the
solid land of the possible, and have put out to sea, where we see the
works of the Lord, and His wonders in the deep. When we think of impossibilities in other spheres we start back; but the way of the Cross is
ablaze with the divine, and we soon perceive that "with God all things
are possible." See, then, in the death of Jesus the possibility of the impossible! Behold here how the Son of God can die. We sometimes

pause when we meet with an expression in a hymn which implies that God can suffer or die; we think that the poet has used too great a license: yet it behooves us to refrain from hypercriticism, since in Holy Writ there are words like it. We even read (Acts 20:28) of "the church of God which he hath purchased with his own blood"—the blood of God! Ah well! I am not careful to defend the language of the Holy Spirit; but in its presence I take liberty to justify the words which we sang just now:

> Well might the sun in darkness hide,
> And shut his glories in,
> When God, the mighty Maker, died
> For man, the creature's sin.

I will not venture to explain the death of the incarnate God. I am content to believe it, and to rest my hope upon it.

How should the Holy One have sin laid upon Him? That also I do not know. A wise man has told us, as if it were an axiom, that the imputation or the nonimputation of sin is an impossibility. Be it so: we have become familiar with such things since we have beheld the truths to us. The doctrine of the Cross is to them that perish foolishness. We do know that in our Lord was no sin, and yet He His own self bare our sins in His own body on the tree. We do not know how the innocent Son of God could be permitted to suffer for sins that were not His own; it amazes us that justice should permit one so perfectly holy to be forsaken of His God, and to cry out, "Eloi, Eloi, lama sabachthani?" But it was so; and it was so by the decree of the highest eclipsed when it was impossible that he should be eclipsed, so has Jesus performed on our behalf, in the agonies of His death, things which, in the ordinary judgment of men, must be set down as utterly impossible. Our faith is at home in wonderland, where the Lord's thoughts are seen to be as high above our thoughts as the heavens are above the earth.

Concerning this miracle, I have also further to remark that *this darkening of the sun surpassed all ordinary and natural eclipses*. It lasted longer than an ordinary eclipse, and it came in a different manner. According to Luke, the darkness all over the land came first, and the sun was darkened afterward: the darkness did not begin with the sun, but mastered the sun. It was unique and supernatural. Now, among all griefs no grief is comparable to the grief of Jesus; of all woes none can parallel the woes of our great Substitute. As strongest light casts deepest shade, so has the surprising love of Jesus cost Him a death such as falls not to the common lot of men. Others die, but this man is "obedient unto death." Others drink the fatal draught, yet reek not of it wormwood and gall; but he "tasted death." "He poured out his soul unto death." Every part of His being was darkened with that extraordinary death-shade; and the natural darkness outside of Him did but shroud a special death which was entirely by itself.

And now, when I come to think of it, *this darkness appears to have been most natural and fitting*. If we had to write out the story of our Lord's death we could not omit the darkness without neglecting a most important item. The darkness seems a part of the natural furniture of that great transaction. Read the story through and you are not at all startled with the darkness; after once familiarizing your mind with the thought that this is the Son of God, and that He stretches His hands to the cruel death of the cross, you do not wonder at the rending of the veil of the temple; you are not astonished at the earthquake or at the rising of certain of the dead. These are proper attendants of our Lord's passion; and so is the darkness. It drops into its place, it seems as if it could not have been otherwise.

> That sacrifice!—the death of him—
> The high and ever Holy One!
> Well may the conscious heaven grow dim,
> And blacken the beholding sun.

For a moment think again. Has not it appeared as if the death which that darkness shrouded was also a natural part of the great whole? We have grown at last to feel as if the death of the Christ of God were an integral part of human history. You cannot take it out of man's chronicle, can you? Introduce the Fall, and see Paradise lost, and you cannot make the poem complete until you have introduced that greater Man who did redeem us, and by His death gave us our Paradise regained. It is a singular characteristic of all true miracles, that though your wonder never ceases they never appear to be unnatural: they are marvelous, but never monstrous. The miracles of Christ dovetail into the general run of human history: we cannot see how the Lord could be on earth and Lazarus not be raised from the dead when the grief of Martha and Mary had told its tale. We cannot see how the disciples could have been tempest-tossed on the Lake of Galilee and the Christ not walk on the water to deliver them. Wonders of power are expected parts of the narrative where Jesus is. Everything fits into its place with surrounding facts. A Romish miracle is always monstrous and devoid of harmony with all beside it. What if St. Winifred's head did come up from the well and speak from the coping to the astonished peasant who was about to draw water! I do not care whether it did or did not; it does not alter history a bit, nor even color it; it is tagged on to the record, and is no part of it. But the miracles of Jesus, this of the darkness among them, are essential to human history; especially is this so in the case of His death and this great darkness which shrouded it. All things in human story converge to the Cross, which seems not to be an afterthought nor an expedient, but the fit and foreordained channel through which love should run to guilty men.

I cannot say more from want of voice, though I had many more things to say. Sit down, and let the thick darkness cover you until you cannot even see the Cross, and only know that out of reach of mortal eye your Lord wrought out the redemption of His people. He wrought in silence a miracle of patience and of love, by which light has come to those who sit in darkness and in the valley of the shadow of death.

A Veil Which Conceals

The Christ is hanging on yonder tree. I see the dreadful cross. I can see the thieves on either side. I look around, and I sorrowfully mark that motley group of citizens from Jerusalem, and scribes, and priests, and strangers from different countries, mingled with Roman soldiers. They turn their eyes on Him, and for the most part gaze with cruel scorn upon the Holy One who is in the center. In truth it is an awful sight. Mark those dogs of the common sort and those bulls of Bashan of more notable rank, who all unite to dishonor the meek and the lowly One. I must confess I never read the story of the Master's death, knowing what I do of the pain of crucifixion, without deep anguish: crucifixion was a death worthy to have been invented by devils. The pain which it involved was immeasurable; I will not torture you by describing it. I know dear hearts that cannot read of it without tears, and without lying awake for nights afterward.

But there was more than anguish upon Calvary: ridicule and contempt embittered all. Those jests, those cruel gibes, those mockeries, those thrustings out of the tongue, what shall we say of these? At times I have felt some little sympathy with the French prince who cried, "If I had been there with my guards, I would soon have swept those wretches away." It was too terrible a sight: the pain of the victim was grievous enough, but the abominable wickedness of the mockers, who could bear? Let us thank God that in the middle of the crime there came down a darkness which rendered it impossible for them to go further with it. Jesus must die; for His pains there must be no alleviation, and from death there must be for Him no deliverance; but the scoffers must be silenced. Most effectually their mouths were closed by the dense darkness which shut them in.

What I see in that veil is, first of all, that it was *a concealment for those guilty enemies*. Did you ever think of that? It is as if God Himself said, "I cannot bear it. I will not see this infamy! Descend, O veil!" Down fell the heavy shades.

I asked the heavens, "What foe to God hath done
This unexampled deed?" The heavens exclaim,
"'Twas man; and we in horror snatched the sun
From such a spectacle of guilt and shame."

Thank God, the Cross is a hiding place. It furnishes for guilty men a shelter from the all-seeing eye, so that justice need not see and strike. When God lifts up His Son, and makes Him visible, He hides the sin of men. He says that "the times of their ignorance he winks at." Even the greatness of their sin He casts behind His back, so that He need not see it, but may indulge His long-suffering, and permit His pity to endure their provocations. It must have grieved the heart of the eternal God to see such wanton cruelty of men toward Him who went about doing good, and healing all manner of diseases. It was horrible to see the teachers of the people rejecting Him with scorn, the seed of Israel, who ought to have accepted Him as their Messiah, casting Him out as a thing despised and abhorred. I therefore feel gratitude to God for bidding that darkness cover all the land, and end that shameful scene. I would say to any guilty ones here: Thank God that the Lord Jesus has made it possible for your sins to be hidden more completely than by thick darkness. Thank God that in Christ He does not see you with that stern eye of justice which would involve your destruction. Had not Jesus interposed, whose death you have despised, you had wrought out in your own death the result of your own sin long ago; but for your Lord's sake you are allowed to live as if God did not see you. This long-suffering is meant to bring you to repentance. Will you not come?

But, further, that darkness was *a sacred concealment for the blessed Person of our divine Lord*. So to speak, the angels found for their King a pavilion of thick clouds, in the which His Majesty might be sheltered in its hour of misery. It was too much for wicked eyes to gaze so rudely on that immaculate Person. Had not His enemies stripped Him naked, and cast lots upon His vesture? Therefore it was meet that the holy manhood should at length find suitable concealment. It was not fit that brutal eyes should see the lines made upon that blessed form by the graving tool of sorrow. It was not meet that revelers should see the contortions of that sacred frame, indwelt with Deity, while He was being broken beneath the iron rod of divine wrath on our behalf. It was meet that God should cover Him, so that none should see all He did and all He bare when He was made sin for us. I bless God devoutly for thus hiding my Lord away: thus was He screened from eyes which were not fit to see the sun much less to look upon the Sun of Righteousness.

This darkness also warns us, even us who are most reverent. This darkness tells us all that *the Passion is a great mystery, into which we cannot pry.* I try to explain it as substitution, and I feel that where the language of Scripture is explicit, I may and must be explicit too. But yet I feel that the idea of substitution does not cover the whole of the matter, and that no human conception can completely grasp the whole of the dread mystery. It was wrought in darkness, because the full, far reaching meaning and result cannot be beheld of finite mind. Tell me the death of the Lord Jesus was a grand example of self-sacrifice—I can see *that* and much more. Tell me it was a wondrous obedience to the will of God—I can see *that* and much more. Tell me it was the bearing of what ought to have been borne by myriad sinners of the human race, as the chastisement of their sin—I can see *that* and I found my best hope upon it. But do not tell me that this is all that is in the Cross. No, great as this would be, there is much more in our Redeemer's death. God only knows the love of God: Christ only knows all that He accomplished when He bowed His head and gave up the ghost. There are common mysteries of nature into which it were irreverence to pry, but this is a divine mystery, before which we put our shoes from off our feet, for the place called Calvary is holy ground. God veiled the cross in darkness, and in darkness much of its deeper meaning lies; not because God would not reveal it, but because we have not capacity enough to discern it all. God was manifest in the flesh, and in that human flesh He put away sin by His own sacrifice: this we all know; but "without controversy great is the mystery of godliness."

Once again, this veil of darkness also pictures to me the way in which *the powers of darkness will always endeavor to conceal the Cross of Christ.* We fight with darkness when we try to preach the Cross. "This is your hour, and the power of darkness," said Christ; and I doubt not that the infernal hosts made in that hour a fierce assault upon the spirit or our Lord. Thus much also we know, that if the Prince of Darkness be anywhere in force, it is sure to be where Christ is lifted up. To becloud the Cross is the grand object of the enemy of souls. Did you ever notice it? These fellows who hate the Gospel will let every other doctrine pass muster; but if the atonement be preached, and the truths which grow out of it, straightway they are aroused. Nothing provokes the Devil like the Cross. Modern theology has for its main object the obscuration of the doctrine of atonement. These modern cuttlefishes make the water of life black with their ink. They make out sin to be a trifle, and the punishment of it to be a temporary business; thus they degrade the remedy by underrating the disease. We are not ignorant of their devices. Expect, my brethren, that the clouds of darkness will gather as to a center around the Cross, that they may hide it from the sinner's view. But expect this also, there is the light eternal of the undying Son of God, who having risen from the dead, lives forever to scatter the darkness of evil.

A Symbol Which Instructs

The veil falls down and conceals, but at the same time, as an emblem, it reveals. It seems to say, "Attempt not to search within, but learn from the veil itself: it hath cherub work upon it." This darkness teaches us what Jesus suffered; it aids us to guess at the griefs which we may not actually see.

The darkness is the symbol of *the wrath of God which fell on those who slew His only begotten Son.* God was angry, and His frown removed the light of day. Well might He be angry, when sin was murdering His only Son; when the Jewish husbandmen were saying, "This is the heir; come, let us kill him, and let us seize on his inheritance." This is God's wrath toward all mankind, for practically all men concurred in the death of Jesus. That wrath has brought men into darkness; they are ignorant, blinded, bewildered. They have come to love darkness rather than light because their deeds are evil. In that darkness they do not repent, but go on to reject the Christ of God. In this darkness God cannot look upon them in complacency, but He views them as children of darkness, and heirs of wrath, for whom is reserved the blackness of darkness forever.

The symbol also tells us *what our Lord Jesus Christ endured.* The darkness outside of Him was the figure of the darkness that was within Him. In Gethsemane a thick darkness fell upon our Lord's spirit. He was "exceeding sorrowful, even unto death." His joy was communion with God—that joy was gone, and He was in the dark. His day was the light of His Father's face: that face was hidden and a terrible night gathered around Him. Brothers, I should sin against that veil if I were to pretend that I could tell you what the sorrow was which oppressed the Savior's soul: only so far can I speak as it has been given me to have fellowship with Him in His sufferings. Have you ever felt a deep and overwhelming horror of sin—your own sin and the sins of others? Have you ever seen sin in the light of God's love? Has it ever darkly hovered over your sensitive conscience? Has an unknown sense of wrath crept over you like midnight gloom, and has it been about you, around you, above you, and within you? Have you felt shut up in your feebleness, and yet shut out from God? Have you looked around and found no help, no comfort even in God—no hope, no peace? In all this you have sipped a little of that salt sea into which our Lord was cast. If like Abraham, you have felt a horror of great darkness creep over you, then have you had a taste of what your divine Lord suffered when it pleased the Father to bruise Him and to put Him to grief. This it was that made Him sweat great drops of blood falling to the ground; and this it was which on the cross made Him utter that appalling cry, "My God, my God, why hast thou forsaken me?" It was not the crown of thorns, or the scourge, or the cross which made Him cry, but the darkness, the awful darkness of desertion which oppressed His mind and made Him feel like one distraught. All that could comfort Him was withdrawn, and all that could distress Him was piled upon Him. "The spirit of a man will sustain his infirmity; but a wounded spirit who can bear?" Our Savior's spirit was wounded, and He cried, "My heart is like wax; it is melted in the midst of my bowels." Of all natural and spiritual comfort He was bereft, and His distress was utter and entire. The darkness of Calvary did not, like all ordinary night, reveal the stars, but it darkened every lamp of heaven. His strong crying and tears denoted the deep sorrow of His soul. He bore all it was possible for His capacious mind to bear, though enlarged and invigorated by union with the Godhead. He bore the equivalent of hell; no, not that only, but He bore that which stood instead of ten thousand hells so far as the vindication of the law is concerned. Our Lord rendered in His death agony an homage to justice far greater than if a world had been doomed to destruction. When I have said that, what more can I say? Well may I tell you that this unutterable darkness, this hiding of the Divine face, expresses more of the woes of Jesus than words can ever tell.

Again, I think I see in that darkness, also *what it was the Jesus was battling with*; for we must never forget that the cross was a battlefield to Him, wherein He triumphed gloriously. He was fighting then with darkness; with the powers of darkness of which Satan is the head; with the darkness of human ignorance, depravity, and falsehood. The battle thus apparent at Golgotha has been raging ever since. Then was the conflict at its height, for the chiefs of the two great armies met in personal conflict. The present battle in which you and I take our little share is as nothing compared with that wherein all the powers of darkness in their dense battalions hurled themselves against the almighty Son of God. He bore their onset, endured the tremendous shock of their assault, and in the end, with shout of victory, He led captivity captive. He by His power and Godhead turned midnight into day again, and brought back to this world a reign of light which, blessed be God, shall never come to a close. Come to battle again, hosts of darkness, if you dare! The Cross has defeated you; the Cross shall defeat you. Hallelujah! The Cross is the ensign of victory; its light is the death of darkness. The Cross is the lighthouse which guides poor weather-beaten humanity into the harbor of peace; this is the lamp which shines over the door of the great Father's house to lead His prodigals home.

Let us not be afraid of all the darkness which besets us on our way home, since Jesus is the light which conquers it all.

The darkness never came to an end until the Lord Jesus broke the silence. All had been still, and the darkness had grown terrible. At last He spoke, and His voice uttered a psalm. It was the Twenty-second Psalm. "My God," says He, "my God, why hast thou forsaken me?" Each repeated "Eloi" flashed morning upon the scene. By the time He had uttered the cry "Why hast thou forsaken me?" men had begun to see again, and some even ventured to misinterpret His words, more in terror than in ignorance. They said, "He calleth Elias"; they may have meant a mock, but I think not. At any rate there was no heart in what they said, nor in the reply of their fellows. Yet the light had come by which they could see to dip the sponge in vinegar. Brethren, no light will ever come to darken hearts unless Jesus shall speak, and the light will not be clear until we hear the voice of His sorrows on our behalf, as He cries, "Why hast thou forsaken me?" His voice of grief must be the end of our griefs; His cry out of the darkness must cheer away our gloom, and bring the heavenly morning to our minds.

You see how much there is in my text. It is a joy to speak on such a theme when one is in good health, and full of vigor; then are we are Naphtali, a hind let loose; then give we goodly words; but this day I am in pain as to my body, and my mind seems frozen. Nevertheless, the Lord can bless my feeble words, and make you see that in this darkness there is meaning deep and wide which none of us should neglect. If God shall help your meditations this darkness will be light about you.

A Sympathy Which Prophesies

Do you see the sympathy of nature with her Lord—the sympathy of the sun in the heavens with the Sun of Righteousness? It was not possible for Him by whom all things were made to be in darkness, and for nature to remain in the light.

The first sympathetic fact I see is this: *all lights are dim when Christ shines not*. All is dark when He does not shine. In the church, if Jesus be not there, what is there? The sun itself could not yield us light if Jesus were withdrawn. The seven golden lamps are ready to go out unless He walks among them, and trims them with the holy oil. Brethren, you soon grow heavy, and your spirits faint, and your hands are weary, if the Christ be not with you. If Jesus Christ be not fully preached, if He be not with us by His Spirit, then everything is in darkness. Obscure the Cross, and you have obscured all spiritual teaching. You cannot say, "We will be perspicuous in every other point, and clear upon every other doctrine, but we will shun the Atonement, since so many cavil at it. No, sirs, if that candle be put under a bushel the whole house is dark.

All theology sympathizes with the Cross, and is colored and tinctured by it. Your pious service, your books, your public worship, will all be in sympathy with the Cross is one way or another. If the Cross in the dark, so will all your work be.

> What think ye of Christ? is the test
> > To try both your work and your scheme;
> You cannot be right in the rest,
> > Unless you think rightly of him.

Conjure up your doubts; fabricate your philosophies; compose your theories; there will be no light in them if the Cross be left out. Vain are the sparks of your own making, you shall lie down in sorrow. All our work and travail shall end in vanity unless the work and travail of Christ be our first and sole hope. If you are dark upon that point which alone is light, how great is your darkness!

Next, *see the dependence of all creation upon Christ*, as evidenced by its darkness when He withdraws. It was not meet that He who made all worlds should die, and yet all worlds should go on just as they had done. If He suffers eclipse, they must suffer eclipse too; if the Son of Righteousness be made to set in blood, the natural sun must keep touch with Him. I believe, my friends, that there is a much more wonderful sympathy between Christ and the world of nature than any of us have ever dreamed. The whole creation groans and travails in pain together until now, because Christ in the church is in His travail pangs. Christ in His mystical body is in travail, and so the whole creation must wait for the manifestation of the Son of God. We are waiting for the coming of the Lord from heaven, and there is no hill or dale, there is no mountain or sea, but what is in perfect harmony with the waiting church. Wonder not that there should be earthquakes in divers places, blazing volcanoes, terrible tempests, and sore spreadings of deadly disease. Marvel not when you hear of dire portents, and things that make one's heart to quail, for such things must be until the end shall come. Until the great Shepherd shall make His crook into a scepter, and shall begin His unsuffering reign, this poor earth must bleed at every vein. There must be darkness until these days of delay are ended. You that expect placid history until Christ shall come expect you know not what. You that think that generous politics shall create order and content, and that the extension of free trade shall breathe universal peace over the nations, look for the living among the dead. Until the Lord shall come, the word has gone out, "Overturn, overturn, overturn," and overturned all things must be, not only in other kingdoms, but in this also, until Jesus comes. All that can be shaken shall be shaken, and only His immovable throne and truth shall abide. Now is the time of the Lord's battle with darkness, and we may not hope as yet for unbroken light.

Dear friends, the sin which darkened Christ and made Him die in the dark darkens the whole world. The sin that darkened Christ and made Him hang upon the cross in the dark is darkening you who do not believe in Him, and you will live in the dark and die in the dark unless you get to Him who only is the light of the world, and can give light to you. There is no light for any man except in Christ, and until you believe in Him thick darkness shall blind you, and you shall stumble in it and perish. That is the lesson I would have you learn.

Another practical lesson is this: If we are in the dark at this time, if our spirits are sunk in gloom, let us not despair, for the Lord Christ Himself was there. If I have fallen into misery on account of sin, let me not give up all hope, for the Father's Well-beloved passed through denser darkness than mine. O believing soul, if you are in the dark you are near the King's cellars, and there are wines on the lees well refined lying there. You have gotten into the pavilion of the Lord, and now may you speak with Him. You will not find Christ in the gaudy tents of pride, nor in the foul haunts of wickedness; you will not find Him where the viol, and the dance, and the flowing bowl inflame the lusts of men, but in the house of mourning you will meet the Man of Sorrows. He is not where Herodias dances, nor where Bernice displays her charms; but He is where the woman of a sorrowful spirit moves her lips in prayer. He is never absent where penitence sits in darkness and bewails her faults.

> Yes, Lord, in hours of gloom,
> When shadows fill my room,
> When pain breathes forth its groans,
> And grief its sighs and moans,
> Then thou art near.

If you are under a cloud, feel after your Lord, if haply you may find Him. Stand still in your black sorrow, and say, "O Lord, the preacher tells me that Your cross once stood in such darkness as this—O Jesus hear me!" He will respond to you; the Lord will look out of the pillar of cloud, and shed a light upon you. "I know their sorrows," says He. He is no stranger to heartbreak. Christ also once suffered for sin. Trust Him, and He will cause His light to shine upon you. Lean upon Him, and He will bring you up out of the gloomy wilderness into the land of rest. God help you to do so!

Last Monday I was cheered beyond all I can tell you by a letter from a brother who had been restored to life, light, and liberty by the discourse of last Sabbath morning. I know no greater joy than to be useful to your souls. For this reason, I have tried to preach this morning, though I am quite unfit for it physically. Oh, I do pray I may hear more news from saved ones! Oh that some spirit that has wandered out into the dark moorland may spy the candle in my window, and find its way home! If you have found my Lord, I charge you never let Him go, but cleave to Him until the day break, and the shadows flee away. God help you so to do for Jesus' sake! Amen.

12

The Tomb of Jesus

Come, see the place where the Lord lay (Matthew 28:6).

Every circumstance connected with the life of Christ is deeply interesting to the Christian mind. Wherever we behold our Savior, He is well worthy of our notice,

> His cross, his manger, and his crown,
> Are big with glories yet unknown.

All His weary pilgrimage, from Bethlehem's manger to Calvary's cross, is in our eyes, paved with glory. Each spot upon which He trod, is to our souls consecrated at once, simply because there the foot of earth's Savior and our own Redeemer once was placed. When He comes to Calvary the interest thickens, then our best thoughts are centered on Him in the agonies of crucifixion, nor does our deep affection permit us to leave Him, even when, the struggle being over, He yields up the Spirit. His body, when it is taken down from the tree, still is lovely in our eyes—we fondly linger around the motionless clay. By faith we discern Joseph of Arimathea, and the timid Nicodemus, assisted by those holy women, drawing out the nails and taking down the mangled body; we behold them wrapping Him in clean white linen, hastily girding Him around with belts of spices, then putting Him in His tomb, and departing for the Sabbath rest. We shall on this occasion go where Mary went on the morning of the first day of the week, when waking from her couch before the dawn, she aroused herself to be early at the sepulcher of Jesus. We will try if it be possible, by the help of God's Spirit, to go as she did—not in body, but in soul—we will stand at that tomb; we will examine it, and we trust we shall hear some truth-speaking voice coming from its hollow bosom which will comfort and in-

---

This sermon was taken from *The New Park Street Pulpit* and was preached on Sunday morning, April 8, 1855.

struct us, so that we may say of the grave of Jesus when we go away, "It was none other than the gate of heaven"—a sacred place, deeply solemn, and sanctified by the slain body of our precious Savior.

An Invitation Given

I shall commence my remarks this morning, by inviting all Christians to come with me to the tomb of Jesus. "Come, see the place where the Lord lay." We will labor to render the place attractive, we will gently take your hand to guide you to it, and may it please our Master to make our hearts burn within us, while we talk by the way.

Away, profane souls whose life is laughter, folly, and mirth! Away, sordid and carnal minds who have no taste for the spiritual, no delight in the celestial. We ask not your company; we speak to God's beloved, to the heirs of heaven, to the sanctified, the redeemed, the pure in heart—and we say to them, "Come, see the place where the Lord lay."

Surely you need no argument to move your feet in the direction of the holy sepulcher, but still we will use the utmost power to draw your spirit thither. Come then, for 'tis the *shrine of greatness*, 'tis the resting place of *the man*, the Restorer of our race, the Conqueror of death and hell. Men will travel hundreds of miles to behold the place where a poet first breathed the air of earth; they will journey to the ancient tombs of mighty heroes, or the graves of men renowned, but where shall the Christian go to find the grave of one so famous as was Jesus? Ask me the greatest man who ever lived—I tell you the Man Christ Jesus, was "anointed with the oil of gladness above his fellows." If you seek a chamber honored as the resting place of genius, turn in here; if you would worship at the grave of holiness, come here; if you would see the hallowed spot where the choicest bones that ever were fashioned lay for awhile, come with me, Christian, to that quiet garden, hard by the walls of Jerusalem.

Come with me, moreover, because *it is the tomb of your best friend*. The Jews said of Mary, "She goeth unto his grave to weep there." You have lost your friends, some of you, you have planted flowers upon their tombs, you go and sit in the evening upon the green sward, bedewing the grass with your tears, for there your mother lies, and there your father, or your wife. Oh! in pensive sorrow come with me to this dark garden of our Savior's burial; come to the grave of your best friend—your brother, yes, one who "sticketh closer than a brother." Come to the grave of your dearest relative, O Christian, for Jesus is Your husband, "Thy Maker is thy husband, the Lord of Hosts is his name." Does not affection draw you? Do not the sweet lips of love woo you? Is not the place sanctified where one so well-beloved slept, although but for a moment? Surely you need no eloquence; if it were needed I have none. I have but the power, in simple, but earnest accents, to repeat the words, "Come, see the place where the Lord lay." On this Easter morning pay a visit to His grave, for it is the grave of your best friend.

Yes, more, I will further urge you to this pious pilgrimage. *Come, for angels bid you.* Angels said, "Come, see the place where the Lord lay." The Syriac version reads, "Come, see the place where *our* Lord lay." Yes, angels put themselves with those poor women, and used one common pronoun—*our*. Jesus is the Lord of angels as well as of men. You feeble women—you have called Him Lord, you have washed His feet, you have provided for His wants, you have hung upon His lips to catch His honeyed sentences, you have sat entranced beneath His mighty eloquence; you call Him Master and Lord, and you do well. "But," said the seraph, "He is my Lord too"; bowing his head, he sweetly said, "Come, see the place where *our* Lord lay." Do you fear then, Christian, to step into that tomb? Do you dread to enter there, when the angel points with his finger and says, "Come, we will go together, angels and men, and see the royal bedchamber"? You know that angels did go into His tomb, for they sat one at His head and the other at His feet in holy meditation. I picture to myself those bright cherubs sitting there talking to one another. One of them said, "it was there His feet lay"; and the other replied, "And there His hands, and there His head"; and in celestial language did they talk concerning the deep things of God; then they stooped and kissed the rocky floor, made sacred to the angels themselves, not because there they were redeemed, but because there their Master and their Monarch, whose high behests they were obeying, did for awhile become the slave of death, and the captive of destruction. Come, Christian, then, for angels are the porters to unbar the door; come, for a cherub is your messenger to usher you into the death place of death himself. No, start not from the entrance; let not the darkness frighten you; the vault is not damp with the vapors of death, nor does the air contain aught of contagion. Come, for it is a pure and healthy place. Fear not to enter that tomb. I will admit that catacombs are not the places where we, who are full of joy, would love to go. There is something gloomy and noisome about a vault. There are noxious smells of corruption; oftentimes pestilence is born where a dead body has lain; but fear it not, Christian, for Christ was not left in hell—in hades—neither did His body see corruption. Come, there is no scent, yes, rather a perfume. Step in here, and, if you did ever breathe the gales of Ceylon, or winds from the groves of Araby, you shall find them far excelled by that sweet holy fragrance left by the blessed body of Jesus, that alabaster vase which once held divinity, and was rendered sweet and precious thereby. Think not that you shall find it obnoxious to your senses.

Corruption Jesus never saw; no worms ever devoured His flesh; no rottenness ever entered into His bones; He saw no corruption. Three days He slumbered, but not long enough to putrefy; He soon arose, perfect as when He entered, uninjured as when His limbs were composed for their slumber. Come then, Christian, summon up your thoughts, gather all your powers; here is a sweet invitation, let me press it again. Let me lead you by the hand of meditation, my brother; let me take you by the arm of your fancy, and let me again say to you, "Come, see the place where the Lord lay."

There is yet one reason more why I would have thee visit this royal sepulcher—*because it is a quiet spot.* Oh! I have longed for rest, for I have heard this world's rumors in my ears so long, that I have begged for "A lodge in some vast wilderness, some boundless contiguity of shade," where I might hide myself forever. I am sick of this tiring and trying life; my frame is weary, my soul is mad to repose herself awhile. I wish I could lie myself down a little by the edge of some pebbly brook, with no companion save the fair flowers or the nodding willows. I wish I could recline in stillness, where the air brings balm to the tormented brain, where there is no murmur save the hum of the summer bee, no whisper save that of the zephyrs, and no song except the caroling of the lark. I wish I could be at ease for a moment. I have become a man of the world; my brain is racked, my soul is tired. Oh! would you be quiet, Christian? Merchant, would you rest from your toils? Would you be calm for once? Then come here. It is in a pleasant garden, far from the hum of Jerusalem; the noise and din of business will not reach you there; "Come, see the place where the Lord lay." It is a sweet resting spot, a withdrawing room for your soul, where you may brush your garments from dust of earth and muse awhile in peace.

Attention Requested

Thus I have pressed the invitation: now we will enter the tomb. Let us examine it with deep attention, noticing every circumstance connected with it.

And first, mark that *it is a costly tomb.* It is no common grave; it is not an excavation dug out by the spade for a pauper in which to hide the last remains of his miserable and overwearied bones. It is a princely tomb; it was made of marble, cut in the side of a hill. Stand here, believer, and ask why Jesus had such a costly sepulcher. He had no elegant garments; He wore a coat without seam, woven from the top throughout, without an atom of embroidery. He owned no sumptuous palace, for He had not where to lay His head. His sandals were not rich with gold, or studded with brilliants. He was poor. Why, then, does He lie in a noble grave? We answer, for this reason: Christ was unhonored until He had finished His sufferings; Christ's body suffered contumely, shame, spitting, buffeting, and reproach, until He had completed His great work; He was trampled under foot, He was "despised and rejected of men; a man of sorrows, and acquainted with grief;" but the moment He had finished His undertaking, God said, "No more shall that body be disgraced; if it is to sleep, let it slumber in an honorable grave; if it is to rest, let nobles bury it; let Joseph, the counselor, and Nicodemus, the man of Sanhedrim, be present at the funeral; let the body be embalmed with precious spices, let it have honor; it has had enough of contumely, and shame, and reproach, and buffeting; let it now be treated with respect." Christian, do you discern the meaning; Jesus after He had finished His work, slept in a costly grave, for now His Father loved and honored Him, since His work was done.

But though it is a costly grave, *it is a borrowed one*. I see over the top of it, "Sacred to the memory of the family of Joseph of Arimathea;" yet Jesus slept there. Yes, He was buried in another's sepulcher. He who had no house of His own, and rested in the habitation of other men; who had no table, but lived upon the hospitality of His disciples; who borrowed boats in which to preach, and had not anything in the wide world, was obliged to have a tomb from charity. Oh! should not the poor take courage? They dread to be buried at the expense of their neighbors; but if their poverty be unavoidable, wherefore should they blush, since Jesus Christ Himself was interred in another's grave? Ah! I wish I might have had Joseph's grave, to let Jesus be buried in it. Good Joseph thought he had cut it out for himself; and that he should lay his bones there. He had it excavated as a family vault, and lo, the Son of David makes it one of the tombs of the kings. But he did not lose it by lending it to the Lord: rather, he had it back with precious interest. He only lent it three days, then Christ resigned it; He had not injured, but perfumed and sanctified it, and made it far more holy, so that it would be an honor in future to be buried there. It was a borrowed tomb; and why? I take it not to dishonor Christ, but in order to show that as His sins were borrowed sins, so His burial was in a borrowed grave. Christ had no transgressions of His own; He took ours upon His head; He never committed a wrong, but He took all my sin, and all yours, if you are believers. Concerning all His people, it is true, He bore their griefs and carried their sorrows in His own body on the tree; therefore, as they were others' sins, so He rested in another's grave; as they were sins imputed, so that grave was only imputedly His. It was not His sepulcher; it was the tomb of Joseph.

Let us not weary in this pious investigation, but with fixed attention observe everything connected with this holy spot. The grave, we observe, *was cut in a rock*. Why was this? The Rock of ages was buried in a rock—a Rock within a rock. But why? Most persons suggest that it was so ordained that it might be clear that there was no covert way by which the disciples or others could enter and steal the body away. Very possibly it was the reason; but oh! my soul, can you not find a spiritual reason? Christ's sepulcher was cut in a rock. It was not cut in mold that might be worn away by the water, or might crumble and fall into decay. The sepulcher stands, I believe, entire to this day; if it does not naturally, it does spiritually. The same sepulcher which took the sins of Paul, shall take my iniquities into its bosom; for if I ever lose my guilt, it must roll off my shoulders into the sepulcher. It was cut in a rock, so that if a sinner were saved a thousand years ago, I too can be delivered, for it is a rocky sepulcher where sin was buried—it was a rocky sepulcher of marble where my crimes were laid forever—buried never to have a resurrection.

You will mark, moreover, that tomb was *one wherein no other man had ever lain.* Christopher Ness says, "When Christ was born He lay in a virgin's womb, and when He died He was placed in a virgin tomb; He slept where never man had slept before." The reason was, that none might say that another person rose, for there never had been any other body there; thus a mistake of persons was impossible. Nor could it be said that some old prophet was interred in the place, and that Christ rose because He had touched his bones. You remember when Elisha was buried, and as they were burying a man, behold he touched the prophet's bones and arose. Christ touched no prophet's bones, for none had ever slept there; it was a new chamber, where the Monarch of the earth did take His rest for three days and three nights.

We have learned a little, then, with attention, but let us stoop down once more before we leave the grave, and notice something else. We see the grave, but do you *notice the grave clothes,* all wrapped and laid in their places, the napkin being folded up by itself? Wherefore are the grave clothes wrapped up? The Jews said robbers had abstracted the body; but if so, surely they would have stolen the clothes; they would never have thought of wrapping them up and laying them down so carefully; they would be too much in haste to think of it. Why was it then? To manifest to us that Christ did not come out in a hurried manner. He slept until the last moment; then He awoke: He came not in haste. They shall not come out in haste, neither by flight, but at the appointed moment shall His people come to Him. So at the precise hour, the decreed instant, Jesus Christ leisurely awoke, took off His cerements, left them all behind Him, and came forth in His pure and naked innocence, perhaps to show us that as clothes are the offspring of sin—when sin was atoned for by Christ, He left all raiment behind Him—for garments are the badges of guilt: if we had not been guilty we should never have needed them.

Then, the napkin, mark you, was laid by itself. The grave clothes were left behind for every departed Christian to wear. The bed of death is well-sheeted with the garments of Jesus, but the napkin was laid by itself because the Christian when he dies, does not need that; it is used by the mourners, and the mourners only. We shall all wear grave clothes, but we shall not need the napkin. When our friends die, the napkin is laid aside for us to use; but do our ascended brothers and sisters use it? No; the Lord God has wiped away all tears from their eyes. We stand and view the corpses of the dear departed, we moisten their faces with our tears, letting whole showers of grief fall on their heads; but do *they* weep? Oh, no, could they speak to us from the upper spheres, they would say, "Weep not for me, for I am glorified. Sorrow not for me; I have left a bad world behind me, and have entered into a far better." They have no napkin—they weep not. Strange it is that those who endure death weep not; but those who see them die are weepers. When the child is born it weeps while others smile (say the Arabs), and when it dies it smiles while others weep. It is so with the Christian. O blessed thing! The napkin is laid by itself, because Christians will never want to use it when they die.

Emotion Excited

We have thus surveyed the grave with deep attention, and, I hope, with some profit to ourselves. But that is not all. I love a religion which consists, in a great measure, of emotion. Now, if I had power, like a master, I would touch the strings of your hearts, and fetch a glorious tune of solemn music from them, for this is a deeply solemn place into which I have conducted you.

First, I would bid you stand and see the place where the Lord lay with *emotions of deep sorrow*. O come, my beloved brother, your Jesus once lay there. He was a murdered man, my soul, and you the murderer.

> Ah, you, my sins, my cruel sins,
> His chief tormentors were,
> Each of my crimes became a nail,
> And unbelief the spear.
>
> Alas! and did my Savior bleed?
> And did my Sov'reign die?

I slew Him—this right hand struck the dagger to His heart. My deeds slew Christ. Alas! I slew my best beloved; I killed Him who loved me with an everlasting love. Eyes, why do you refuse to weep when you see Jesus' body mangled and torn? Oh! give vent to your sorrow, Christians, for you have good reason to do so. I believe in what Hart says, that there was a time in his experience when he could so sympathize with Christ that he felt more grief at the death of Christ than he did joy. It seemed so sad a thing that Christ should have to die; and to me it often appears too great a price for Jesus Christ to purchase worms with His own blood. I think I love Him so much that if I had seen Him about to suffer, I would have been as bad as Peter, and have said, "That be far from thee, Lord;" but then He would have said to me, "Get thee behind me, Satan;" for He does not approve of that love which would stop Him from dying. "The cup which my Father hath given me, shall I not drink it?" But I think, had I seen Him going up to His cross, I could fain have pressed Him back, and said, "Oh! Jesus, You shall not die; I cannot have it. Will You purchase my life with a price so dear?" It seems too costly for Him who is the prince of life and glory to let His fair limbs lie tortured in agony; that the hands which carried mercies should be pierced with accursed nails; that the temples that were always clothed with love should have cruel thorns driven through them. It appears too much. Oh! weep, Christian, and let your sorrow rise. Is not the price all but too great, that your Beloved should for you resign *Himself*. Oh! I should think if a person were saved from death by another, he would always feel deep grief if his deliverer lost his life in the attempt. I had a friend, who, standing by the side of a piece of frozen water, saw a young lad in it, and sprang upon the ice in order to save him. After clutching the boy he held him in his hands, and cried out, "Here he is! here he is! I have saved him." But just as they caught hold of the boy, he himself sank and his body was not found for some time afterward when he was quite dead. Oh! it is so with Jesus. My soul was drowning. From heaven's high portals He saw me sinking in the depths of hell. He plunged in.

> He sank beneath his heavy woes,
>   To raise me to a crown;
> There's ne'er a gift his hand bestow;
>   But cost his heart a groan.

Ah! we may indeed regret our sin, since it slew Jesus.

Now, Christian, change your note a moment. "Come, see the place where the Lord lay," *with joy and gladness.* He does not lie there now. Weep, when you see the tomb of Christ, but rejoice because it is empty. Your sin slew Him, but His divinity raised Him up. Your guilt has murdered Him, but His righteousness has restored Him. Oh! He has burst the bonds of death; He has ungirt the cerements of the tomb, and has come out more than conqueror, crushing death beneath His feet. Rejoice, O Christian, for He is not there—He is risen. "Come, see the place where the Lord lay."

One more thought, and then I will speak a little concerning the doctrines we may learn from this grave. "Come, see the place where the Lord lay" *with solemn awe*, for you and I will have to lie there too.

> Hark! from the tomb a doleful sound,
>   Mine ears, attend the cry;
> Ye living men, come view the ground,
>   Where ye must shortly lie.

> Princes, this clay must be your bed,
>   In spite of all your powers;
> The tall, the wise, the reverend head,
>   Must lie as low as ours.

It is a fact we do not often think of, that we shall all be dead in a little while. I know that I am made of dust and not of iron; my bones are not brass, nor my sinews steel: in a little while my body must crumble back to its native elements. But do you ever try to picture to yourself the moment of your dissolution? My friends, there are some of you who seldom realize how old you are, how near you are to death. One way of remembering our age is to see how much remains. Think how old eighty is, and then see how few years there are before you will get there. We should remember our frailty. Sometimes I have tried to think of the time of my departure. I do not know whether I shall die a violent death or not; but I wish to God that I might die suddenly, for sudden death is sudden glory. I wish I might have such a blessed exit as Doctor Beaumont, and die in my pulpit, laying down my body with my charge, and ceasing at once to work and live. But it is not mine to choose. Suppose I lie lingering for weeks in the midst of pains, and griefs, and agonies; when that moment comes, that moment which is too solemn for my lips to speak of, when the spirit leaves the clay—let the physician put it off for weeks or years, as we say he does, though he does not—when that moment comes, oh, you lips, be dumb, and profane not its solemnity. When death comes, how is the strong man bowed down. How does the mighty man fall. They may say they will not die, but there is no hope for them; they must yield, the arrow has gone home. I knew a man who was a wicked wretch, and I remember seeing him pace the floor of his bedroom, saying, "O God, I will not die, I will not die." When I begged him to lie on his bed, for he was dying, he said he could not die while he could walk, and he would walk until he did die. Ah! he expired in the utmost torments, always shrieking, "O God, I will not die." Oh! that moment, that last moment. See how clammy is the sweat upon the brow, how dry the tongue, how parched the lips. The man shuts his eyes and slumbers, then opens them again; and if he be a Christian, I can fancy he will say:

> Hark! they whisper: angels say
> Sister spirit, come away.
> What is this absorbs me quite—
> Steals my senses—shuts my sight—
> Drowns my spirit—draws my breath?
> Tell me, my soul, can this be death?

We know not when he is dying. One gentle sigh, and the spirit breaks away. We can scarcely say, "He is gone," before the ransomed spirit takes its mansion near the throne. Come to Christ's tomb then, for the silent vault must soon be your habitation. Come to Christ's grave, for you must slumber there. And even you, sinners, for one moment I will ask you to come also, because you must die as well as the rest of us. Your sins cannot keep you from the jaws of death. I say, sinner, I want you to look at Christ's sepulcher too, for when you die it may have done you great good to think of it. You have heard of Queen Elizabeth crying out that she would give an empire for a single hour; or, have you read the despairing cry of the gentleman on board the *Arctic,* when it was going down, who shouted to the boat, "Come back! I will give you £30,000 if you will come and take me in." Ah! poor man, it were but little if he had thirty thousand worlds, if he could thereby prolong his life, "Skin for skin; yes, all that a man hath will he give for his life." Some of you who can laugh this morning, who came to spend a merry hour in this hall, will lie dying, and then you will pray and crave for life, and shriek for another Sabbath day. Oh! how the Sabbaths you have wasted will walk like ghosts before you! Oh! how they will shake their snaky hair in your eyes! How will you be made to sorrow and weep, because you wasted precious hours, which, when they are gone, are gone too far ever to be recalled. May God save you from the pangs of remorse.

Instruction Imparted

And now, Christian brethren, "Come, see the place where the Lord lay," to learn a doctrine or two. What did you see when you visited "the place where the Lord lay?" "He is not here: for he is risen." The first thing you perceive, if you stand by His empty tomb, is *His divinity*. The dead in Christ shall rise first at the resurrection; but He who rose first— their leader, rose in a different fashion. They rise by imparted power. He rose by His own. He could not slumber in the grave, because He was God. Death had no more dominion over Him. There is no better proof of Christ's divinity than that startling resurrection of His, when He rose from the grave, by the glory of the Father. O Christian, your Jesus is a God; His broad shoulders that hold you up are indeed divine;

and here you have the best proof of it—because He rose from the grave.

A second doctrine here taught, well may charm you, if the Holy Spirit apply it with power. Behold this empty tomb, O true believer: it is a sign of *your acquittal* and your full discharge. If Jesus had not paid the debt, He would never have risen from the grave. He would have lain there until this moment if He had not canceled the entire debt, by satisfying eternal vengeance. Oh! beloved, is not that an overwhelming thought?

> It is finished! It is finished!
> Hear the rising Savior cry.

The heavenly turnkey came; a bright angel stepped from heaven and rolled away the stone. But he would not have done so if Christ had not done all; he would have kept Him there; he would have said, "No, no, You are the sinner now; You have the sins of all Your elect upon Your shoulder, and I will not let You go free until You have paid the uttermost farthing." In His going free I see my own discharge. "My Jesu's blood's my full discharge."

As a justified man, I have not a sin against me in God's book. If I were to turn over God's eternal book I should see every debt of mine receipted and canceled.

> Here's pardon for transgressions past,
> It matters not how black their cast,
> And O my soul with wonder view,
> For sins to come here's pardon too.
> While through thy blood absolved I am
> From sin's tremendous curse and blame.

One more doctrine we learn, and with that we will conclude—*the doctrine of the Resurrection.* Jesus rose, and as the Lord our Savior rose, so all His followers must rise. Die I must—this body must be a carnival for worms; it must be eaten by those tiny cannibals; peradventure it shall be scattered from one portion of the earth to another; the constituent particles of this my frame will enter into plants, from plants pass into animals, and thus be carried into far distant realms; but at the blast of the archangel's trumpet every separate atom of my body shall find its fellow; like the bones lying in the valley of vision, though separated from one another, the moment God shall speak, the bone will creep to its bone; then the flesh shall come upon it; the four winds of heaven shall blow, and the breath shall return. So, let me die, let beasts devour me, let fire turn this body into gas and vapor, all its particles shall yet again be restored; this very selfsame actual body shall start up from its grave, glorified and made like Christ's body, yet still the same body, for God has said it. Christ's same body rose: so shall mine. O my soul, do you now dread to die? You will lose your partner body a little while, but you will be married again in heaven; soul and body shall again be united before the throne of God.

The grave—what is it? It is the bath in which the Christian puts the clothes of his body to have them washed and cleansed. Death—what is it? It is the waiting room where we robe ourselves for immortality; it is the place where the body, like Esther, bathes itself in spices, that it may be fit for the embrace of its Lord. Death is the gate of life; I will not fear to die, then, but will say,

> Shudder not to pass the stream,
> Venture all thy care on him—
> Him, whose dying love and power
> Still'd its tossing, hush'd its roar;
> Safe is the expanded wave,
> Gentle as a summers eve;
> Not one object of his care
> Ever suffer'd shipwreck there!

Come view the place, then, with all-hallowed meditation, where the Lord lay. Spend this afternoon, my beloved brethren, in meditating upon it, and very often go to Christ's grave both to weep and to rejoice. You timid ones, do not be afraid to approach, for 'tis no vain thing to remember that timidity buried Christ. Faith would not have given Him a funeral at all; faith would have kept Him above ground, and would never have let Him buried, for it would have said it would be useless to bury Christ if He were to rise. Fear buried Him. Nicodemus, the night disciple, and Joseph of Arimathea, secretly, for fear of the Jews, went and buried Him. Therefore, you timid ones, you may go too. Ready-to-halt, poor Fearing, and you Mrs. Despondency, and Much-afraid, go often there; let it be your favorite haunt, there build a tabernacle, there abide. And often say to your heart, when you are in distress and sorrow, "Come, see the place where the Lord lay."